Around the Table

Around the Table
ELLEN WRIGHT
EASY MENUS FOR COZY ENTERTAINING AT HOME

PHOTOGRAPHY BY TOM ECKERLE

THE HARVARD COMMON PRESS

BOSTON, MASSACHUSETTS

THE HARVARD COMMON PRESS
535 ALBANY STREET
BOSTON, MASSACHUSETTS 02118
WWW.HARVARDCOMMONPRESS.COM

Text © 2003 by Ellen Wright
Photography © 2003 by Tom Eckerle

Printed in China
Printed on acid-free paper

Library of Congress Cataloging-in-Publication Data

Wright, Ellen.
    Around the table : easy menus for cozy entertaining at home / Ellen Wright ; photography by
Tom Eckerle.
       p. cm.
    ISBN 1-55832-252-3 (hc: alk. paper)
1. Entertaining. 2. Cookery. 3. Menus. I. Title.
    TX731.W732 2003
    642'.4—dc21   2003002443

Special bulk-order discounts are available on this and other Harvard Common Press books.
Companies and organizations may purchase books for premiums or resale, or may arrange
a custom edition, by contacting the Marketing Director at the address above.

10   9   8   7   6   5   4   3   2   1

BOOK DESIGN BY DEBORAH KERNER / DANCING BEARS DESIGN

DEDICATED TO

MY MOTHER,

ALWAYS SMART

AND CAPABLE,

WITH THE HIGHEST STANDARDS

Contents

Cold Weather Menus

Warm Weather Menus

Acknowledgments

Special thanks to:

- Jessica Benjamin, my niece and friend and editor, who extracted more information than I ever knew I had and without whom I couldn't have written this book

- My wonderful husband, Joe

- My loving children, Claudia and Andrew, Alexis and Bill, David and Celine

- My grandchildren, Julia, Allie, Jonny, Kelsey, Charlotte, and Cate

- Carla Glasser, my agent, who always "gets it"

- Pam Hoenig, my editor, who is always supportive

- Tom Eckerle, my good friend and fantastic photographer

- Rena, Roscoe, and their style

- All my testers: Jessica Benjamin, Meg Bloom, Julie Coburn, Joslyn Hills, Gerri Jansen, Carla Jegan, Mike Klecan, Gerda McDonough, Claudia Plepler, Alexis Proceller, Monika Rozek, Theresa Viellecazes, and Joe Wright

- All the contributors, who are mentioned for each and every recipe, changed or unchanged

Introduction

When it comes to really enjoying a meal, there's no place like home. When people come to my house to eat, I always try to make sure they feel welcome, are in a comfortable setting, and are entertained with lively conversation and, of course, memorable food. It's not about impressing my guests; in fact, almost the opposite is true. It's about making them feel at home.

The first thing people see when they come through my front door is my "welcome kitty." In Asia, it is traditional to have one of these waving cats greet anyone who arrives and, conversely, wish them well when they leave and remind them to come back. I love my little welcome kitty. It puts a smile on everyone's face.

I always have a dish filled with lemon drops by the front door so people can help themselves. My little grandchildren and nieces and nephews ask where the candy is if they don't see any. The grownups do, too, so I am careful to keep the dish well stocked. It's become my signature, like wearing a particular perfume.

Home is where the kitty and the lemon drops are, you could say, but home is also where you invite friends and family in for a meal. One of my favorite places to entertain is the kitchen. No matter how big or beautiful your house is, everyone seems to gravitate to the kitchen. Even if it's tiny, friends manage to squeeze in while you are cooking. It is the hub of the house. I think it makes people feel part of the family, part of the "doing." If you have an eat-in kitchen, you know how wonderful it is to cook and talk to your guests while you are preparing food or clearing the table and cleaning up. The host used to be more isolated; now she or he is an integral part of the party. No one expects you to cook behind a "curtain" anymore, to present a meal out of nowhere on a silver platter.

I have found that the more involved guests are, the more at home they feel. People don't mind pitching in family style—tossing the salad or helping to serve the dessert. It not only helps me out, but it makes them feel as if this is "our" meal.

The most important rule I have found about entertaining at home is to be yourself. If you are comfortable in your own skin, your guests will be relaxed as well. That doesn't mean you need to shy away from trying new recipes or cooking dishes that challenge you. It does mean that you should plan your meal and be in control—although, goodness knows, we are all human and mistakes do happen. But if you don't let little—or even disastrous—mishaps bother you, they won't bother your guests. The important thing is, no matter the situation, that you do the best you can. The rest is about getting people together and having fun.

It can be frightening to invite a group of people whom you want to impress, or at least stay friends with, into your home. But it is important to keep calm and let your own style come through.

I am not a restaurant chef, a caterer, or a professional party-giver, but I have been cooking and entertaining for more than 40 years. I started in my early 20s, as an art student in California, when I was studying painting and pottery at Mills College. Working with my hands gave me the confidence to work with any and all recipes, including difficult pastry dough. I watched one demonstration by Julia Child, then bought cookbooks and food magazines, trying any recipe that caught my eye. Probably youthful arrogance was as much the key to my training as anything else, because I didn't think twice about inviting friends over to try my first go at a soufflé or puff pastry or French crepes. I had no fear and gained confidence by cooking and entertaining. I made mistakes but never felt beaten by them. It always made me try the dish again.

Having moved many times—16 to be exact—I have learned to be flexible. I also have learned what's important, and I have decided that ease and friendship are it. I know how to set up a comfortable home and begin entertaining for new friends because I have had to do it time after time.

In the late 1960s and early 1970s, I entertained a great deal for fundraising purposes. For several years, I had formal sit-down dinners once a month for 22 people. At the end of six months, I had cooked for more than 130 people. By this time, I had three young children at home. It didn't faze me. I loved to cook and bake, and I had lots of energy. I organized my time so that I could do everything.

During the early 1970s, I met the great James Beard at a dinner party. Sitting across from each other, we talked during the meal about everything to do with food: where he bought his eggs and butter, his favorite recipes, ways of entertaining and cooking. The meal we were eating was terrible in every way: too complicated, too fancy, too pretentious, and not at all tasty. At the end of the evening, as we were leaving, I invited him to dinner. He looked stunned, saying, "No one ever invites me to dinner." It struck me then that famous people, and particularly good cooks or chefs, intimidate others and tend to be left out. People are afraid to invite them to their homes.

We became close friends, and I studied cooking with him for seven years, working as an assistant, testing for his cookbooks, and doing some demonstrations with him. I threw Jim a party for his 75th birthday at my home. He invited about 20 friends, and I served a wonderful dinner and a

big bottle of Perrier-Jouet champagne. At the end of the meal, he stood up to give a toast, which included thanking me for the celebration. He said, "Ellen, you are a very good cook, although there are better cooks than you, and you are a good baker, but there are also some better than you. But I don't know anyone who is better at bringing people together, making them feel at home, and serving a damn good meal."

My own philosophy about entertaining is this: keep it simple, don't complicate anything, and enjoy your own evening. Here is what I like to think of as my "10 commandments" of a successful get-together.

1. The most important decision is the guest list. Think of your guests the way you think of a recipe: you want balance; a good mixture of people. Mix old friends with new faces—it's always more interesting that way. I try to mix intense with laid-back, well-off with struggling, artists with businesspeople, lawyers with writers. People are people, and everyone has something to offer. It works.

2. Make what *you* want to eat. It should be simple, good food, not pretentious. Don't tie yourself in knots trying to figure out what *they* want to eat. If you please yourself, everyone else will be happy. When I feel like eating Basque Chicken, for example, I decide to have a party because it's so great for a crowd.

3. Get as much work done ahead of time as possible. Cook and freeze, chop and prep. Flowers, music, napkins, and the look of the table are all things you can deal with early.

4. Plan the table setting with interesting combinations of dishes, glasses, and napkins. Don't be afraid to combine unusual items. Things don't need to match or be perfect. Try something a little different as a centerpiece, such as a music box or a pretty sculpture, or use an unusual place card holder, such as a pinecone. Think about ways to give out "grown-up" party favors, such as pretty shells you collected on the beach or bags of jellybeans tied up with ribbon—something fun.

5. Don't put anything too fragrant or too high on the table. Flowers and candles should be low and have no smell. Food is coming, and you don't want anything competing or clashing with those aromas. Float flowers in a large, shallow dish, or use several tiny bud vases or pitchers around the table.

6. Music should be in the background and not compete with conversation. Jazz, guitar, or classical music creates an atmosphere and enhances the connection you are making with your guests and they with one another. Music should not intrude. Never play vocals; words fight words.

7. Make your cocktail hour short and sweet. Sitting down, talking intimately at the table, is where you want to spend most of your time. You don't want to stand up for a long time, and you don't want to be too full to enjoy dinner.

8. Don't be shy. Ask your friends to pass a course or a plate or to fill a wineglass. Treat everyone as you do your family. Include them in the meal. Don't leave anyone out. Make everyone feel needed as a bartender or host. Your friends will be fine with that. In fact, they will enjoy it.

9. Always serve dessert at the table. Once your guests get up, dinner is over—in my house, anyway.

10. End the night early enough for guests to feel free to go. I knew one host who used to excuse himself early and go to bed. Everyone is happy to get together and also happy to return to the quiet of his or her own home after a good meal with friends. Don't feel you have to carry on forever.

I always try to create a balance when coming up with a menu. I want foods that will marry well and harmonize but not necessarily be matched perfectly. I think about color, taste, texture, hot/cold, spicy/sweet. I don't want a meal that is all white or all brown or all anything. If garlic is prominent in one recipe, it can't be in another. Put tomatoes in one dish, but not two. I try to make it simple, not complicated. If the flavors are competing, you won't be able to taste a thing. I never have too many herbs in a dish. I want one chewy recipe served with one soft dish, one crunchy vegetable with something creamy. I like a light dessert with a big fancy dinner, or a drop-dead dessert with a very simple meal.

I have written this cookbook in menu form for this reason: it makes it easier to use for those who need to know how to combine food, and it allows more experienced cooks to change things around and substitute to their hearts' content.

When people have had dinner at my house, they always seem happy to come back. I don't think it's because I serve the fanciest meals or uncork the most expensive wines. I think it is because I make them feel at home.

When you are putting together a dinner party, brunch, or barbecue, remember why you wanted to do it in the first place. Most often, you want to bring people together. If you lose sight of that by getting bogged down with menu or décor or flowers, you won't be able to have fun.

As a long-time decorator, I use the same guiding principles when designing a house, apartment, or office. Why do people like my work? What makes my homes and offices look lived in and comfy? I know what goes together, and I begin with that as a foundation. But I mix things up and add surprises to give the feeling of warmth and character. For example, I like to paint the back of my bookcases a random color to add something unusual behind the books. If everything in a room is beige and you paint the backs of the bookcases a bright Chinese red or teal blue, it adds a little unexpected interest to the room.

You should do the same with your table. Your everyday dishes and your formal "wedding" china are like the basics of your wardrobe: jeans and white T-shirt, little black dress. The fun comes in adding the accessories. Start by collecting odd platters from flea markets or old salad plates from your mother or grandmother. These accents can add so much. I also love to take something traditionally used for one purpose and use it for a totally different purpose. I often serve heavy cream or raspberry sauce for dessert in a clear glass bud vase or use demitasse cups for soup instead of coffee. If you try something a little unexpected, such as fruit instead of flowers or seashells or pinecones for your centerpiece, it will have a big impact.

If you make your table and your home cozy and inviting, people will want to come back again and again.

Just like home.

My Larder

People have said to me, "What is a larder? What is in a larder? Why do you have so many things in your larder?" My answer is that when I have surprise company or I run out of ideas for dinner or lunch, I go to my kitchen cabinet (or larder) and it helps me, providing ingredi-

ents and inspiration for a variety of easy meals. I
am grateful for it all the time.

In the cabinet:
  Pasta
  Canned tomatoes, whole and crushed
  Canned or jarred tomato sauce
  Anchovies
  Pitted black olives
  Capers
  Tuna, solid white albacore in water
  Canned beef broth or beef bouillon cubes
  Canned chicken broth or chicken bouillon cubes
  Canned cannellini beans or chickpeas
  Canned petite peas
  Red wine vinegar and/or balsamic vinegar
  Oyster sauce
  Soy sauce
  Toasted sesame oil
  Olive oil
  Canola oil
  Chili oil
  Tabasco sauce
  Taco kit: taco sauce, taco shells,
    canned green chiles
  Golden raisins
  Canned juices (pineapple, apricot, tomato)
  Saltines

In the fridge:
  Cheese (Muenster, cheddar)
  Butter

Sour cream
  Mayonnaise
  Hot cherry peppers in a jar
  Soft flour and corn tortillas
  Strawberry or apricot preserves
  Mustard (several kinds)
  Baking potatoes
  Onions
  Garlic
  Lemons or lemon juice

In the freezer:
  Fordhook lima beans
  Chopped spinach
  Artichoke hearts
  Peasant bread
  Bacon and/or breakfast sausage
  Raspberries
  Phyllo pastry

For baking:
  Sugar
  Confectioners' sugar
  Brown sugar, light and dark
  All-purpose flour
  Wondra flour
  Semisweet chocolate bits
  Unsweetened cocoa powder
  Baking powder (lasts only 3 to 6 months)
  Baking soda
  Yellow cake mix
  Lemon-flavored instant pudding
  Vegetable shortening

Cold Weather Menus

When Labor Day has passed and you traditionally can't wear white linen anymore, I start to think about entertaining for the fall. It usually takes me a while to recover from the summer, when I have had just about enough of everything: corn and tomatoes, gardening and harvesting, sun and beach towels and lots of company.

Fall is definitely my favorite season. I love the colors and the smells, the trees changing, the beginning of school and the end of vacation. I love to watch how the vibrant pinks, clear yellows, and bright reds yield to golds, apricots, rusts, and burgundies. I watch the pumpkins and gourds start to appear, piling up in various shapes and sizes.

This is the time of year I used to buy my girls little plaid dresses with white collars and brand-new Bonnie Doon knee socks for going back to school. Fall is about reconnecting with friends after a long summer away and even starting to plan the upcoming holidays, which don't seem so far off on the calendar.

Once my mind starts to adapt to the change of season, I start to think of tastes, flavors, and colors I want to have. Because the food at this time of year is meant to warm you up, my menus are filled with roasts and stews, thick soups, and cobblers.

When the weather turns really cold, I want to huddle by the fireplace or gather with friends and family in my warm kitchen. I also think of dressing differently. One great thing about cold weather is putting on jeans and a soft sweater—something cozy and casual.

The way you "dress" your table sets the tone as well. When the weather is brisk and chilly, I rely less on cut flowers. Instead, I use pinecones, gourds, and pots of chrysanthemums; little wrapped presents around the holidays; and cinnamon or chocolate hearts for Valentine's Day. You can bring warmth to your home and your table simply by adding character.

After a summer of pastels and paper plates, I relish the opportunity to bring out my brown transferware, which features various country scenes. I have almost a complete set of matching dinner plates, along with a selection of odd platters and serving dishes. The browns are all different, but I don't mind that at all. I also purchased a complete knockoff set from a catalog about 10 years ago. It looks as if I've had it forever, passed down through the generations. Maybe that's why it creates such a homey feeling.

I also adore my eBay juice glasses, which I sometimes use in place of large wine goblets. I can mix up the sets, using some with stripes, some with roosters, some with flowers. The men make fun of me, but they like it, too.

On really cold nights, we have a fire going in the fireplace. We keep split logs on our tiny terrace, and my husband, Joe, hauls in 10 at a time in the canvas carrier. While I am putting the finishing touches on dinner, he is busy making a fire fit for a king. Even if we don't eat in front of the fire, we always have a drink or munchies there.

Just because the food at this time of year is hearty doesn't mean it has to be heavy. I like people to leave the table satisfied but not stuffed. One-dish meals, casseroles, and stews are great because you can't get that kind of food anywhere but home.

My First Dinner Party
Impressive for a Crowd

Pistachios and assorted olives

Arugula and Endive Salad

Basque Chicken with Sausage and Tomato
  Pimento Sauce over brown rice

Perfect Lemon Cake with
  Fresh Lemon Glaze

I made this meal for my very first dinner party when I was a 20-year-old student living in Berkeley, California. I invited my neighbors, who also were students. We were all beginning to learn how to cook. I loved figuring out what to make—the more complicated, the better—and going to all the little shops to buy meat, bread, flowers, special spices, vegetables, and fruits. Because I was in art school, learning painting and potting and good with my hands, I was enthusiastic about creating with food. Basque Chicken is inspired by a recipe in Elizabeth David's *French Country*

Cooking, which still sits on my shelf 40 years later—yellowed, pages falling out, and splattered with food.

This is a simple menu: one dish with rice, chicken, sausage, and vegetables, along with a salad and a great dessert. I have a huge, round, hand-thrown pottery platter that was made by one of the graduate students I knew at Mills College named Wayne Taylor, and I always use it to show off this dish. It does my heart good to see my guests digging into the communal pot with gusto.

Arugula and Endive Salad

Makes 8 servings

I like to serve arugula because of its slight bite and good taste. Endive adds a nice crunch and color to the salad. I use an Asian-style dressing here, but this salad also is good with Ellen's Favorite Dressing: Version 1 (page 110).

Salad:

2 Belgian endives

2 bunches arugula

1 medium-size cucumber, peeled and sliced

2 scallions (white and green parts), chopped

Asian dressing:

½ cup olive oil

1 teaspoon sesame oil

2 tablespoons fresh lemon juice

1 tablespoon soy sauce

½ teaspoon sugar

Freshly ground black pepper to taste

1. To make the salad, wash the endives, then core and cut them in half lengthwise. Set aside on paper towels. Wash and dry the arugula, snap off the large stems, and wrap in paper towels to absorb all the water.

2. Tear the large arugula leaves into bite-size pieces. Place in a salad bowl and add the cucumber. Top with the scallions, cover with a clean kitchen towel, and refrigerate until ready to serve.

3. To make the dressing, combine all the ingredients in a jar with a tight-fitting lid. Shake well right before using. Pour over the salad and toss to coat evenly. Serve as soon as possible.

ELLEN'S TIPS

★ You can wrap the greens in paper towels and refrigerate for up to 2 hours.

★ Try this with chopped fresh chives or red onion instead of scallions.

★ You can make the dressing several days ahead of time. I keep some in the cupboard at all times to use as needed (no need to refrigerate).

Basque Chicken with Sausage and Tomato Pimento Sauce

Makes 8 servings

I love this one-dish meal. It is made with sweet sausage and chicken seasoned with thyme and served with brown rice and a sauce of fresh tomatoes and pimentos. The combination of flavors is great. It can be made in advance, and I always reserve the special-tasting chicken stock for a good soup later.

Two 5- to 6-pound chickens, cut
   into serving-size pieces
1 tablespoon ground thyme
Salt and freshly ground black pepper
   to taste
2 medium-size onions, quartered
1 bay leaf
1½ pounds sweet Italian sausages
½ orange

Rice:
   4 cups water
   2 cups brown rice
   2 teaspoons vegetable oil
   Pinch of salt

Sauce:
   8 large ripe tomatoes, cored and cut
      into 2-inch pieces
   2 teaspoons ground thyme
   Salt and freshly ground black pepper
      to taste
   Three 4-ounce jars whole pimentos,
      drained
   1 tablespoon canola oil or bacon fat
   1 tablespoon paprika

   1 tablespoon chopped fresh parsley
      leaves, for garnish

1. Preheat the oven to 400°F.
2. Rinse and dry the chicken pieces. Season on both sides with the thyme and salt and pepper. Put the chicken skin side up in a large casserole and add the onions and bay leaf. Put the sausages on top, then squeeze the orange half over everything and add it to the pot.
3. Bake, uncovered, until the chicken and sausages are browned, about 40 minutes.

Reduce the oven temperature to 350°F and pour in enough water to barely cover the chicken and sausages. Cover and bake until the chicken is practically falling off the bones, 40 to 50 minutes more.

4. To make the rice, bring the water to a boil in a 2-quart saucepan over high heat. Add the rice, oil, and salt. Reduce the heat to medium-low, cover, and cook until dimples show on top of the rice, 20 to 30 minutes. Stir once and turn off the heat.

5. Meanwhile, make the sauce. In a medium-size mixing bowl, toss the tomatoes with the thyme and salt and pepper. Cut the pimentos into ½-inch-wide strips. In a large skillet over medium heat, heat the oil until hot but not smoking. Add the pimentos and cook, stirring, until they lighten in color, about 2 minutes. Add the seasoned tomatoes, cover, and cook until softened, about 12 minutes, stirring with a wooden spoon until the sauce is slightly mixed. Stir in the paprika.

6. Discard the bay leaf and orange from the chicken. Transfer the chicken to a serving platter and keep warm. Slice the sausages into 1-inch-thick rounds and add to the chicken. Strain the broth through a fine-mesh strainer and set aside. Discard any loose bones, skin, and cartilage.

7. To serve, place the rice in a mound in the center of a large platter. Add a ladleful of the chicken broth to moisten it. Arrange the chicken and sausage pieces around the rice. Spoon some of the sauce over the chicken and sausage and sprinkle the rice with the parsley. Serve the remaining sauce on the side.

ELLEN'S TIPS

★ If you are one of those people who save bacon fat, it is wonderful in this dish. Just spread some on the chicken pieces before baking and remember to omit any salt if you use it.

★ Do not overcook the sauce: it should resemble tomato pieces and pimento strips.

Perfect Lemon Cake with
Fresh Lemon Glaze

Makes 8 to 10 servings

★ If the cake breaks while you are unmolding it, take the pieces out and place them in their rightful positions. When you glaze the cake, the breaks won't show.

★ Serve the cake warm, if possible. It's divine that way.

★ This cake can be made the day before. I keep it on a covered cake plate. You also could invert a bowl over the cake when completely cooled.

This is an adaptation of a recipe given to me a long time ago by a friend in San Francisco. It is moist and velvety, travels well, and is great to bring to any dinner. In short, it is a wonderful cake worth knowing. As for the cake and pudding mixes, I am not above using shortcuts to achieve good results.

Cake:

1 package yellow cake mix
1 package lemon-flavored instant pudding
4 large eggs, at room temperature
¾ cup canola oil
½ cup water

¼ cup sweet sherry, port, or orange juice
1 teaspoon freshly grated nutmeg

Lemon glaze:

1 cup confectioners' sugar
1 to 2 tablespoons fresh lemon juice

1. Preheat the oven to 350°F. Grease and flour a bundt pan, knocking out the excess flour.

2. To make the cake, in a large mixing bowl with an electric mixer on medium speed, beat the cake mix, pudding, eggs, oil, water, sherry, and nutmeg until very smooth and thick, at least 5 minutes.

3. Pour the batter into the prepared pan and bake in the middle of the oven until the sides of the cake pull away from the pan and a skewer inserted in the center comes out clean, about 45 minutes.

4. Remove from the oven and let cool on a wire rack for 10 minutes. While it is cooling, make the glaze. Place the confectioners' sugar in a small mixing bowl and add the lemon juice a little at a time, mixing with a fork until smooth. Set aside.

5. Using a sharp knife, loosen the sides of the cake from the pan until you can unmold it easily onto a cake plate. While the cake is still warm but not hot, drizzle the glaze over the cake.

The Sopranos on Trays

My Favorite Show of the Week

Quesadilla Triangles

Baked Potatoes with Stir-Fried Chicken
and Veggies

Mixed Greens, Tomatoes, and Cukes

Toffee Bars with Crumbled Candy

On Sunday night, we try not to miss our favorite television show—*The Sopranos,* on HBO. This meal is perfect because it's easy to eat on a tray. And for the times when television really is the priority, we bring out our old set of hand-painted TV tables. They come in handy when you want to enjoy a meal without balancing it on your lap. This meal doesn't require cutting, so you can keep your eyes glued to the set. The stir-fry filling can be made ahead of time, in the afternoon, and reheated just before serving. The only task you have at the last minute is to cut open the baked potatoes and slice the iceberg lettuce for the stir-fry. Dessert should be made in the morning.

Quesadilla Triangles

Makes 6 to 8 servings

I could eat a whole batch of these in one sitting! In fact, I have made a meal out of them. Here I use them as a munchie before the show starts. I also serve them for lunch, cut into bigger wedges. They are so simple and taste great.

1 to 2 tablespoons canola oil, as needed
Four 6-inch soft flour tortillas

½ cup shredded Muenster cheese
2 green chiles (canned are best), cut into thin strips

1. In a small skillet over high heat, heat 1 tablespoon of the canola oil until hot but not smoking. Reduce the heat to medium and place 1 tortilla in the pan. Place 2 tablespoons of cheese in the middle and top with a few strips of chile. Top with another tortilla and press the edges together as the quesadilla cooks. Brown one side, then turn over and brown the other, about 2 minutes per side. Transfer to a plate and repeat with the remaining tortillas and filling, using the remaining oil, if necessary.
2. Cut into wedges and serve.

ELLEN'S TIPS

★ If you don't have chiles on hand, sprinkle red pepper flakes over the cheese. Or use jalapeño Muenster cheese, which already has the hot peppers in the cheese.

★ I like to use a cast-iron skillet to make these; they cook so much better that way.

★ If you want a very spicy munchie, use fresh chiles. You also may substitute chopped onion, scallion greens, or fresh cilantro leaves for the chiles.

Baked Potatoes with Stir-Fried Chicken and Veggies

Makes 2 to 4 servings

★ You may substitute any vegetable or meat for those I suggest. For vegetables, sliced zucchini, broccoli florets, lima beans, and peas are all good. I also have used leftover chicken, pot roast, and sliced steak, as well as leftover noodles. Be creative.

★ You may thicken the gravy with 2 teaspoons cornstarch dissolved in 1/4 cup cold water if you don't have Wondra flour.

I am the queen of stir-fry because it is so easy and quick. I usually have most of these ingredients in my kitchen cabinet and refrigerator. It's also a great way to use up leftovers. I like to serve the stir-fry inside the baked potatoes, although you could use pasta or rice just as well. I use a wok, but a frying pan will do.

Potatoes:
2 to 4 medium-size to large Idaho potatoes
2 tablespoons olive oil
Kosher salt to taste

Stir-fry:
2 tablespoons vegetable oil
1 tablespoon sesame oil
4 to 6 medium-size cloves garlic, crushed
2 medium-size onions, thinly sliced

1 teaspoon red pepper flakes or chili oil (optional)
1 tablespoon oyster sauce
1 whole boneless, skinless chicken breast, cut into 3-inch-long x 1/2-inch-wide strips
1 medium-size ripe tomato, seeded and diced
4 to 6 mushrooms, sliced
2 cups chicken broth
2 cups thinly sliced iceberg lettuce
2 to 3 tablespoons Wondra flour (see note on page 14)

1. Preheat the oven to 400°F.
2. Wash and dry the potatoes. Pierce with a sharp knife or fork in 3 or 4 places. Rub with the olive oil and sprinkle with salt. Bake until the potato skins are crispy and the flesh is tender when pierced with a fork, 40 to 50 minutes. Set aside.
3. To make the stir-fry, heat the vegetable oil and sesame oil together in a wok or large frying pay over medium-high heat. When it is hot but not smoking, add the garlic and onions and stir-fry until lightly browned. Add the red pepper flakes and oyster

sauce and mix. Add the chicken and sear on both sides, about 2 minutes total. (I sear the chicken strips on the sides of the wok, where they stick.) Reduce the heat to medium, add the tomato and mushrooms, and cook for about 1 minute. Add the chicken broth, cover, and simmer for 2 to 3 minutes. Add the lettuce, cover, and simmer until it wilts, about 1 minute.

4. Using a slotted spoon, transfer the chicken and vegetables to a plate. Add the flour to the pan sauce and whisk over medium heat until thickened, about 2 minutes. Return the chicken and vegetables to the pan to keep warm.

5. When ready to serve, transfer the mixture to a serving bowl and let your guests fill their own potatoes.

Wondra Flour

Wondra flour is a granulated flour used for browning and to thicken gravy. It doesn't lump or clump like regular flour. You can find it in the supermarket.

Mixed Greens, Tomatoes, and Cukes

Makes 2 to 4 servings

My mixed greens might not be your mixed greens, and in this recipe, you can substitute whatever you want.

1 head chicory, center leaves only

1 head romaine lettuce, center leaves only

1 medium-size ripe tomato

1 medium-size cucumber (see Ellen's Tips)

½ teaspoon dried basil

½ teaspoon dried oregano

3 tablespoons chopped scallions (white and green parts)

½ cup Ellen's Favorite Dressing: Version 1 (page 110)

1. Wash and dry the lettuce leaves, using only the best part of each head to make enough for 4 people.
2. Wash and core the tomato and cut into wedges.
3. Peel and seed the cucumber, if you need to, then slice.
4. Combine the lettuce, tomato, and cucumber in a salad bowl and add the basil and oregano.
5. When ready to serve, add the scallions. Pour the dressing over all and toss lightly to coat evenly.

★ I know when the shortbread is done because I can smell it. That's not very scientific, but it works with baking most of the time.

★ These bars are best when warm.

Toffee Bars with Crumbled Candy

Makes 24 bars

This toffee shortcake bar evolved from a recipe from my dear friend Meredith, and neither of us can remember where it came from. It is sinful and wonderful. While the shortbread base is still hot, it is topped with crumbled candy—Heath or Skor bars or any praline-type candy, such as Almond Roca. The candy melts enough to make a crunchy, buttery, brown sugar topping. Cut each bar as you eat it, or the bars will dry out.

1 cup (2 sticks) unsalted butter, softened

1 cup firmly packed light or dark brown sugar

1 large egg yolk, at room temperature

1 teaspoon pure vanilla extract

2 cups sifted all-purpose flour

¼ teaspoon salt

3 Heath or Skor bars, broken into 1-inch pieces

Chopped walnuts (optional)

1. Preheat the oven to 350°F. Grease an 8-inch square baking dish.
2. In a large mixing bowl with an electric mixer on high speed, beat the butter, brown sugar, egg yolk, and vanilla until smooth. Reduce the speed to medium-low, add the flour and salt, and beat until the flour disappears.
3. Press the dough evenly into the prepared baking dish. Bake until the shortbread sets, about 25 minutes.
4. Remove from the oven and, while the crust is still hot, sprinkle the candy and the walnuts, if using, evenly over the top. Let cool slightly before cutting.

It's Payback Time
Must-Do Buffet for 10

Parmesan Toasts

Tomato Onion Soup

Glazed Pork Loin with Mustard
  and Brown Sugar

Whole Baked Onions

Boston Lettuce Gratinée

Montana Flood Cake

You know how it is when you've been invited to several dinners but are too busy to have one of your own. You can get away with not having people over for just so long, and then it's time to reciprocate. This is a good opportunity to bring different people together and have some fun.

Autumn is when I want to make this particular meal. The pork loin with prunes lends itself to this time of year, and the brown sugar and mustard glaze adds a new taste dimension. The lettuce gratinée is always a hit—guests love the flavor but cannot figure out what it is. I like to serve this meal on a long sideboard in my living room and then sit down at round tables covered with pretty fall-colored cloths. In the center of each table, I sometimes place a shallow basket filled with pinecones. The pinecones also can be strewn on the tables in an informal way. I make a real effort to make this a special evening for my somewhat forgotten good friends.

Parmesan Toasts

Makes 8 to 10 servings

ELLEN'S TIPS

★ These toasts can be baked in a pre-heated 425°F oven for about 10 minutes, instead of broiling.

★ Italian bread also works well.

These crispy little toasts go well with soups and salads when you want something a little more interesting than croutons. They are not difficult to make and keep well. No matter how many of these I prepare for a get-together, the basket is always empty.

1 loaf French bread, sliced ½ inch thick at an angle
½ cup (1 stick) butter, melted
½ cup freshly grated Parmesan cheese

3 tablespoons chopped fresh parsley leaves (optional), for garnish

1. Preheat the oven to broil.
2. Dip one side of each bread slice into the melted butter. Place the Parmesan cheese on a plate and dredge the buttered bread in the cheese. Put the bread cheese side up on a baking sheet. Broil until golden brown, 2 to 3 minutes. *Stand by the oven while doing this and don't leave*; the toasts will burn if left a second too long.
3. Remove from the oven and garnish with the parsley, if using.

Tomato Onion Soup

Makes 10 small servings

I love this soup for a party and like to serve it in small *demitasse* cups along with the Parmesan Toasts (see previous recipe). It is also great to make in advance and keep frozen; it can be quickly reheated for last-minute meals. You can decorate it with a lemon slice; chopped fresh cilantro leaves, chives, or scallion greens; or even toasted pine nuts.

4 cups crushed tomatoes

1 cup beef broth

1 small onion, stuck with 2 cloves

1 tablespoon chopped fresh basil leaves
   or 1 teaspoon dried

½ teaspoon freshly ground white
   pepper

½ teaspoon baking soda

1½ teaspoons sugar

2 teaspoons all-purpose flour

2 teaspoons butter

3 tablespoons chopped scallions
   (white and green parts),
   for garnish

1. Place the tomatoes, broth, onion, basil, and pepper in a large saucepan. Stir together and bring to a simmer over medium-high heat. Add the baking soda and sugar, reduce the heat to low, cover, and simmer for about 40 minutes. Remove the onion and discard.

2. Using a fork, mash the flour and butter together into a paste on a small plate. Add to the soup, increase the heat to medium, and stir until the soup thickens, about 5 minutes.

3. Serve immediately, garnished with the chopped scallions.

Beurre Manié
   The flour and butter paste used to thicken this soup is also known as beurre manié, *or kneaded butter.*

ELLEN'S TIPS

★ You can use canned whole tomatoes, but remember to break them up with your hands, cut out the blossom ends, and process in a blender or food processor until smooth.

★ This soup is also super served cold.

★ I love to pour this soup, hot or cold, from a pretty china or silver coffeepot with a long spout into different-patterned demitasse cups. People can sip the soup during cocktails as a taste of what's to come.

★ You also may serve the soup as a first course in a proper bowl, but double the recipe if necessary.

Glazed Pork Loin with Mustard and Brown Sugar

Makes 10 servings

★ Some butchers
will lard the pork
loin with the pro-
sciutto for you; ask
them to cut the ham
into finger-sized
strips. It's a great
help if they do.

★ Allow the meat to
cook slowly. If you
try to rush it using
high heat, it will be
tough.

This is the most delicious braised pork because of the combination of ingredients: mustard, brown sugar, and prunes. The pork loin is larded with prosciutto, which gives it a terrific flavor. I learned this recipe 40 years ago from the classic French cookbook by Simone Beck, *Simca's Cuisine*. Beck served it with Boston Lettuce Gratinée (page 24) because the combination is perfect, and I always do, too.

2 cups beef broth

18 medium-size pitted prunes

One 5- to 6-pound pork loin, boned, rolled, and tied (ask your butcher to do this)

¼ pound prosciutto, cut into 3- to 4-inch-long x ½-inch-thick strips

½ cup Dijon mustard

⅔ cup firmly packed dark brown sugar

2 tablespoons canola oil

⅔ cup bourbon

Salt and freshly ground black pepper to taste

1 teaspoon dried thyme

1 teaspoon dried sage

4 sprigs fresh parsley

1 teaspoon cornstarch, dissolved in 2 tablespoons cold water

1 bunch watercress, stems removed, for garnish

1. Preheat the oven to 375°F.
2. Heat 1 cup of the broth in a medium-size saucepan. Add the prunes, remove from the heat, and set aside.
3. Using a sharp knife or long skewer, push the prosciutto strips into the center of the loin lengthwise. Do this from both ends, as they won't go the whole length of the loin. When you slice the braised loin, you will have prosciutto in each slice.
4. Paint the pork loin with the mustard. Place the brown sugar on a plate and roll the pork in it to coat evenly.

Nana's Macaroni and Cheese

Makes 6 to 8 servings

I don't know why macaroni and cheese is so well loved, but it is. It is real comfort food. I have combined many recipes from numerous sources through the years until the best and most straightforward version evolved. I think this is a winner. It encompasses all that's good about a dish that has stood the test of time.

One 16-ounce package elbow macaroni
Salt to taste
1 teaspoon canola oil
3 tablespoons butter
1 cup diced onion
2 tablespoons all-purpose flour
2 cups half-and-half
Freshly ground white pepper
   to taste
2 cups shredded sharp white cheddar
   cheese
½ cup plain dry bread crumbs
¼ cup freshly grated Parmesan cheese

1. Preheat the oven to 350°F.
2. Bring a large saucepan of water to a boil. Add the macaroni, salt, and canola oil and cook until *al dente* (see Ellen's Tips). Drain and set aside.
3. In a large saucepan over medium-high heat, melt 2 tablespoons of the butter. Add the onion and cook, stirring, until transparent, about 5 minutes. Reduce the heat to low, add the flour, and cook until pasty, about 2 minutes. Add the half-and-half and stir until the mixture is smooth. Season with salt and pepper. Remove from the heat and stir in 1½ cups of the cheddar cheese until it melts.
4. In a large mixing bowl, combine the macaroni and cheese sauce and toss until well mixed. Spoon the mixture into a buttered casserole dish and sprinkle the bread crumbs, the remaining ½ cup cheddar, and the Parmesan on top. Dot with the remaining 1 tablespoon of butter and bake until golden brown, 30 to 40 minutes. Serve hot.

PB&Js

Short for peanut butter and jelly sandwiches, this is a recipe for all seasons and all people, big or small, old or young. As far as I am concerned, the sandwiches are best made with chunky peanut butter and strawberry or grape jam on soft, fresh white bread with the crusts removed. They seem to taste better if cut into small and dainty squares.

One fun thing to do for kids is to cut each sandwich in the shape of the first letter of the child's name——J for James and so on. Other shapes also are possible: moons, hearts, chickens, ducks, or just rounds. Use cookie cutters to make the shapes, if you have them.

Best-Ever Egg Salad Sandwiches

Makes 6 to 8 sandwiches

I love my egg salad because it is finely chopped, soft, and smooth. I like it uncluttered with add-ins, and most kids do, too. For grownups, feel free to include chopped celery or onion.

8 large eggs
½ cup mayonnaise
Salt and freshly ground white pepper
  to taste

3 tablespoons finely chopped fresh
  chives (optional)
12 to 18 slices white bread

1. Place the eggs in a medium-size saucepan and add cold water to cover. Bring to a boil over high heat. After 30 seconds, turn off the heat and let sit for 15 to 20 minutes. Remove using a slotted spoon, peel under tepid running water, and dry.
2. Place the eggs in a food processor. Add the mayonnaise and pulse until the eggs are finely chopped but not pureed. Transfer to a large mixing bowl, season with salt and pepper, and fold in the chives, if desired.
3. Spread the egg salad generously on half of the bread slices and top with the remaining slices. Cut off the crusts with a sharp serrated knife, then cut the sandwiches into quarters.
4. Serve immediately or wrap tightly in plastic until ready to serve.

ELLEN'S TIPS

★ If you follow my instructions exactly, you'll end up with beautiful yellow yolks, not greenish ones, which result from overboiling.

★ You can prepare the egg salad a day or two ahead and refrigerate it, tightly covered.

★ Remember not to let eggs and mayonnaise sit in a hot place, such as outside at a picnic, for more than 30 minutes.

Shoestring Potatoes

Makes 6 to 8 servings

These are simply French-fried potatoes that are very thinly cut. Follow the instructions exactly for success.

3 cups canola oil

2 large Idaho potatoes, peeled and cut into thin matchsticks

Sea salt or kosher salt to taste

1. In a large skillet over medium-high heat, heat the canola oil until hot but not smoking.
2. Place small handfuls of the potatoes in the hot oil and cook, turning them with a slotted spoon, until golden brown, about 6 minutes. Using the slotted spoon, transfer the potatoes to generous layers of paper towels to drain.
3. Sprinkle right away with sea salt and serve hot.

Devil's Food Cupcakes with White Icing

Makes 24 medium-size cupcakes

For decorating fun, I set small bowls filled with sprinkles (each bowl with a different color) in a row in the middle of the table. At each end, I have a bowl of icing and a plate of cupcakes. I show the kids how to dip their cupcakes, holding them by the paper bottoms, and twirl them in the soft icing. It may take a couple of tries to get the top fully covered. Then the decorating can begin. Little ones may need some grown-up help.

ELLEN'S TIPS

★ You can use this recipe as is to make a 9 x 13-inch sheet cake. Just increase the baking time to about 1 hour. If you want to make a layer cake, use two or three 9-inch layer pans, dividing the batter evenly between them, and double the amount of icing. Start checking for doneness after about 15 minutes in the oven. Either way, first grease and flour the baking pans.

Devil's food cupcakes:

2 cups granulated sugar
¾ cup vegetable shortening
2 large eggs, at room temperature
3 cups sifted cake flour
½ teaspoon salt
½ cup unsweetened cocoa powder
1 cup buttermilk
2 teaspoons baking soda
1 cup boiling water

White icing:

½ cup (1 stick) unsalted butter, softened
2⅔ cups confectioners' sugar
2 to 4 tablespoons heavy cream, half-and-half, or whole milk, as needed
Pinch of salt
1 teaspoon pure vanilla extract

1. Preheat the oven to 350°F. Place muffin liners in full-size muffin tins.
2. To make the cupcakes, place the granulated sugar and shortening in a large mixing bowl. With an electric mixer on medium speed, cream together until light and fluffy. Add the eggs one at a time, beating well after each addition. In a medium-size mixing bowl, sift together the dry ingredients and add alternately to the egg mixture with the buttermilk.
3. Add the baking soda to the boiling water Add to the batter and mix on low speed until smooth. Spoon the batter into the prepared tins, filling each cup about three-quarters full.

4. Place the muffin tins in the center of the oven and bake until a skewer inserted in the center of a cupcake comes out clean, 15 to 20 minutes. Remove from the oven and let cool completely.

5. To make the icing, place the butter, confectioners' sugar, and 2 tablespoons of the cream in a large mixing bowl. With an electric mixer on low speed, beat until smooth. Add more cream if necessary, a little at a time, to achieve a spreadable consistency. Transfer the icing to 2 bowls and allow the children to frost their own cupcakes, or frost the cupcakes yourself.

Icing Variations:
- *If you want chocolate icing, add ¾ cup unsweetened cocoa powder.*
- *For mocha icing, add 1 tablespoon strong brewed coffee and half the heavy cream.*
- *Use crushed pecans, walnuts, M&M's, or sprinkles to decorate the cupcakes.*

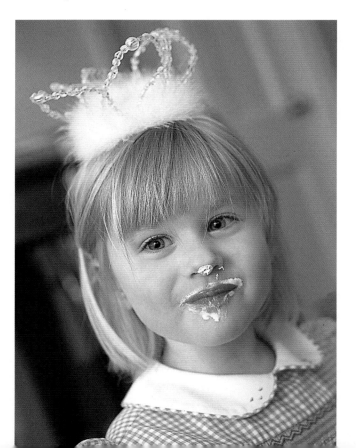

Mini Thanksgiving

For an Abbreviated Gathering

Roquefort Grapes

Cheese Puff Pastry Sticks with Salt

Cranberry Orange Roast Chicken

Laurie's Crunchy Noodle Pudding

Tricolor Vegetable Puree

Joe's Baked Apples and My Piecrust Cookies

This Thanksgiving menu is for a small group, no more than six. My children are all married now, and they alternate Thanksgiving and Christmas with their in-laws. That means every other year, I have a houseful, but other years it's just Joe and I and a few friends. When my children are home, they expect the same dishes they've always had, and there is no hope of deviating. But for the smaller Thanksgiving celebration, I like to try recipes that depart from the traditional foods. I prepared this roast chicken recipe a while ago, making it up as I went along. It is still one of my favorites. Ending with Joe's Baked Apples and My Piecrust Cookies is a twist on "ye olde Thanksgiving pie."

For my table, I mound gourds grown in my garden in a huge Italian bowl painted with a yellow and green design. I like to continue the yellow and green theme in my choice of plates, napkins, and flowers to tie it all together.

Roquefort Grapes

Makes 6 servings

The combination of Roquefort cheese, chopped walnuts, and sweet grapes cannot be beat. It is a perfect one-bite treat with a drink at cocktail time.

18 perfect purple or green seedless grapes

½ cup mashed Roquefort cheese
½ cup walnuts, finely chopped

1. Wash and dry the grapes.
2. Take a bit of the cheese and make a small pancake of it in your hand. Put a grape in the middle of the pancake and wrap it around the grape with your fingers. Work quickly because the heat of your hands may melt the cheese.
3. Roll the grape in the chopped nuts and set on a plate. Repeat with the remaining grapes, cheese, and nuts. Refrigerate, covered with plastic wrap, until ready to serve. Serve cold.

ELLEN'S TIPS

★ You can make these little babies in the morning or the day before, just keep them refrigerated until the party starts.

★ Chopped almonds or pecans also work nicely.

Cheese Puff Pastry Sticks with Salt

Makes 24 sticks

What could be easier than these buttery sticks made out of puff pastry, which is readily available at the grocery store in the refrigerator section? They are sprinkled with grated cheddar cheese and coarse salt and served warm with a glass of cold wine.

1 package puff pastry
½ cup finely shredded sharp white cheddar cheese

2 tablespoons sea salt or kosher salt

1. Preheat the oven to 400°F.
2. Sprinkle 1 pastry sheet evenly with 1 tablespoon of the cheese. Cut into 4-inch-long x ½-inch-wide strips and place on an ungreased cookie sheet. Repeat with the remaining pastry sheet and cheese.
3. Bake on the center oven rack until golden brown, about 10 minutes. Transfer to a plate and sprinkle with the sea salt. Serve warm.

ELLEN'S TIPS

★ These sticks can be stored, tightly wrapped, for several days and then reheated before serving.

★ They also can be frozen this way. Just be sure to defrost them fully before reheating.

★ You can sprinkle them with finely chopped fresh parsley leaves, chives, dill, or sage leaves before baking, if you like. Your own variations are welcome.

★ Seeds, such as caraway, sesame, black mustard, or poppy, can be sprinkled on before baking.

★ When deglazing
the pan, you can add
a few tablespoons of
white wine, if you
wish. A Chardonnay
or a slightly fruity
white is a good
choice. Add the wine
to the pan first,
scraping up the
browned bits, then
add the chicken
broth and continue
as directed.

★ I use Wondra
flour to thicken my
gravy because it
does so without
lumping.

★ Serve the gravy in
a little pitcher or
even a small coffee-
pot.

(continued on page 40)

Cranberry Orange Roast Chicken

Makes 6 to 8 servings

In my family, this chicken is one of our favorites. The citrus berry sauce and orange juice make the skin brown and crunchy, and I have never met anyone who doesn't love that. Although this is perfect for an informal Thanksgiving dinner, it can certainly be served any time of the year. For decoration, I often surround the chicken with whole fresh cranberries, crab apples, pyracantha branches with their orange berries, or even persimmons—depending on what I can get.

One 6-pound or two 4- to 5-pound
   chickens
2 medium-size onions, stuck with
   2 cloves each
3 tablespoons butter
½ cup orange juice, or 1 tablespoon
   frozen orange juice concentrate
   mixed with ½ cup water

1 cup whole-berry cranberry sauce
   (canned is fine)
2 cups chicken broth
2 tablespoons Wondra flour

1. Preheat the oven to 400°F.
2. Rinse the chicken and pat dry. Place on a rack in a roasting pan (if using 2 birds, make sure they don't touch) and put the onions in the pan. Rub the chicken with 2 tablespoons of the butter. Set on the center oven rack and bake for 20 minutes, then reduce the oven temperature to 350°F.
3. Meanwhile, in a measuring cup, mix the orange juice and cranberry sauce together with a fork. Baste the chicken with this mixture every 15 minutes until the mixture is gone. Roast the chicken until it is golden brown and the juices run clear when it is cut at the joint, about 1¼ hours total. Remove from the oven and transfer to a warm plate to rest for 15 minutes.

ELLEN'S TIPS

(continued from page 38)

★ For an extra-spe-
cial touch, I like to
garnish my chicken
with frosted cran-
berries. To do this,
dip fresh cranberries
in beaten egg white,
roll them in granulat-
ed sugar, place on a
tray, and freeze. Set
them around your
bird straight from
the freezer.

4. Over medium heat, using the same roasting pan, add the chicken broth to the chicken juices and slowly deglaze the pan by scraping the browned bits up from the bottom. Add the flour 1 tablespoon at a time to thicken the gravy, whisking constantly. Strain the gravy through a fine-mesh strainer and swirl in the remaining 1 tablespoon butter. Keep warm until ready to serve.

5. Cut the chicken into serving-size pieces and serve with the gravy on the side.

Laurie's Crunchy Noodle Pudding

Makes 8 to 10 servings

This recipe is from my ex-sister-in-law, Laurie, who always gave wonderful dinners with my younger brother, Barry. Her recipe is so good that it remains in our family by popular demand. Noodle pudding can be served with meat, fish, or chicken, or even as a brunch dish. It is slightly sweet and crispy and holds a special place in my repertoire.

Two 16-ounce packages broad
   egg noodles

2 tablespoons margarine

½ cup sugar

Three 3-ounce packages cream
   cheese, softened

5 large eggs

3 cups whole milk

1 tablespoon pure vanilla extract

½ cup golden raisins

½ cup (1 stick) margarine, melted

Topping:

1 cup corn flakes, crushed

1 teaspoon ground cinnamon

1 tablespoon sugar

1 cup canned crushed pineapple,
   drained

1. Preheat the oven to 350°F. Grease a 9 x 13-inch baking dish.
2. Cook the noodles in a pot of lightly salted boiling water with a little oil until soft but not mushy. Drain, return to the pot, and toss with the 2 tablespoons margarine. Set aside.
3. In a large mixing bowl, cream together the sugar and cream cheese. Add the eggs, milk, vanilla, raisins, and melted margarine and mix well. Add the cooked noodles and toss with a wooden spoon. Pour the noodles into the prepared baking dish.
4. To make the topping, combine all the ingredients in a medium-size bowl, mixing well. Spread evenly over the noodles.
5. Bake until the top is golden brown and crunchy, 45 to 60 minutes. Serve hot.

Tricolor Vegetable Puree

Makes 6 to 8 servings

This lovely dish should be baked in a glass soufflé or baking dish that will show off the different colors. It consists of stripes of vegetable purees: green peas and lima beans, orange carrots and yams, and white potatoes and celery root. When you serve it, you get all three layers. This is a perfect accompaniment to any meat, fish, or poultry dish.

ELLEN'S TIPS

★ Fordhook lima beans have more meat and make a better puree than small limas do.

★ Choose a celery root that isn't too beat-up looking. The superficial nicks will peel off, but deeper scars discolor the flesh.

★ Make each puree the consistency of mashed potatoes. Some vegetables have more liquid than others, so you might add less cream. If it gets too thin, reduce the puree in a skillet over low heat to thicken.

Lima and pea puree:

One 10-ounce package frozen lima beans (preferably Fordhook; see Ellen's Tips)
One 8-ounce can petite peas
2 tablespoons butter
2 tablespoons sour cream
Salt and freshly ground white pepper to taste

Carrot and yam puree:

3 medium-size fresh or a 28-ounce can yams, drained
8 medium-size carrots, sliced
3 tablespoons butter
2 to 3 tablespoons sour cream, as needed
Salt and freshly ground white pepper to taste

Potato and celery root puree:

3 large russet potatoes, peeled and cut into 1-inch cubes
1 medium-size celery root, peeled and cut into 1-inch cubes
3 tablespoons butter
2 to 3 tablespoons heavy cream, as needed
Salt and freshly ground white pepper to taste

3 tablespoons chopped fresh chives, parsley or cilantro leaves, or scallions (white and green parts), for garnish

1. To make the lima and pea puree, place the lima beans and peas with their liquid in a medium-size saucepan and heat until boiling. Drain and transfer to a food processor. Add the butter and sour cream and pulse until smooth. Season with salt and pepper. Transfer to a medium-size bowl, cover with plastic wrap, and keep warm.

2. To make the carrot and yam puree using fresh yams, peel them and cut into 2-inch cubes. Place in a medium-size saucepan, add the carrots and water to cover, and bring to a boil. Continue to boil until the vegetables are tender, 12 to 15 minutes. Drain. If using canned yams, cook the carrots by themselves. Place the carrots, yams, and butter in a food processor. Adding the sour cream a little at a time, pulse until smooth. Keep the puree thick. Season with salt and pepper. Transfer to a medium-size bowl, cover with plastic wrap, and keep warm.

3. To make the potato and celery root puree, place the potatoes and celery root in a large saucepan with water to cover and bring to a boil. Reduce the heat to medium and cook until tender, about 30 minutes. Drain and transfer to a food processor. Add the butter and heavy cream and pulse until smooth. Season with salt and pepper. Transfer to a medium-size bowl, cover with plastic wrap, and keep warm.

4. Assemble the purees in a 3-inch-deep glass soufflé or baking dish. Spoon 1 puree into the dish and smooth the top. Add the other 2 purees one at a time, smoothing the top of each. Cover with aluminum foil and keep warm in a 200°F oven for up to 40 minutes.

5. To serve, top with the garnish of your choice.

ELLEN'S TIPS

★ To save some time, make each puree a day or two before and keep refrigerated. On the day of serving, bring to room temperature before assembling. After assembling, cover with aluminum foil and bake in a 300°F oven until heated through, 30 to 40 minutes.

Joe's Baked Apples

Makes 8 servings

There isn't an easier dessert to throw together at the last minute than these baked apples. My husband contributed the way to do this. He cores and bakes them, skin left on, with butter and jam. My addition is a pitcher of cold heavy cream to serve with the warm apples.

8 Rome apples, cored
½ cup strawberry preserves
  (or your favorite)

½ cup (1 stick) unsalted butter
1 cup cold heavy cream,
  for serving

1. Preheat the oven to 350°F.
2. Place the apples in a baking dish large enough to hold them comfortably. Spoon 1 tablespoon preserves and 1 tablespoon butter into the cored-out center of each apple.
3. Bake until bubbly and tender when tested with a sharp knife, 30 to 40 minutes.
4. Serve warm with the heavy cream in a small pitcher for pouring.

ELLEN'S TIPS

★ Other good apple choices are Golden Delicious or McIntosh.

★ Other jams I like are black cherry, blackberry, raspberry, peach, and apricot.

★ Pour the cream out of a bud vase, cruet, or pretty bottle for a change.

My Piecrust Cookies

Makes twenty-four 3-inch cookies

I am a big fan of piecrust cookies. In fact, I have been known to make a batch and devour most of them by myself with a big glass of cold milk. This kind of voracious act is very unlike me, but these funny little cookies have a way of casting a warm and delicious spell.

⅓ cup sugar

½ teaspoon ground cinnamon

1 recipe Foolproof Piecrust (page 83)

1. Preheat the oven to 425°F.
2. Combine the sugar and cinnamon in a small bowl.
3. Turn the piecrust out onto a lightly floured work surface and, using a floured rolling pin, roll it out to about ¼ inch thick. Cut into squares or shapes and sprinkle with the cinnamon sugar. Transfer to ungreased cookie sheets.
4. Bake until golden brown, about 10 minutes. Cool on the sheets, then transfer to a plate.

ELLEN'S TIPS

★ Don't be afraid to touch the dough. You can gently pick it up and turn it when you first roll it to prevent sticking. Use light fingers.

★ If you prepare the dough a day in advance, take it out of the refrigerator and let it warm up for 30 to 40 minutes before rolling it out. This helps to prevent cracking and breaking.

★ Give young children a little of their own dough to work with. They may handle it too much to bake cookies from it, but the dough will keep them very happy for a little while.

Homemade for the Holidays

Cooking Gifts with or Without the Kids

Old-Fashioned Chocolate Chip Cookies

Bessie's Thumbprint Cookies

Apricot Ginger Chutney

Best Homemade Mustard

Berry Crunch Bread

Homemade gifts are so much more appreciated than store-bought ones. And hand-painted presents are even better. Shopping for plaid ribbons and little glass jars in different shapes and sizes is great fun and a good activity for two or even three generations to do together. We have our own little assembly line, and everyone—from the 3-year-olds to the 40-year-olds—has a job. One granddaughter is a master at drawing and painting, so I give her the job of decorating jars and labels. The only grandson in our group loves to fill the jars.

We put the small cookies in unusual containers, such as Shaker wooden boxes, apothecary jars, cookie tins, or even aluminum foil packages done up with pretty ribbon. The bread is best wrapped the same way, in aluminum foil and tied with ribbon. Any 3-year-old can punch out a hole in the recipe card that is attached to each treat so that each recipient can make his or her own next year. We all take turns tying the ribbons into bows and feel quite satisfied with our efforts in this gift-giving enterprise.

Old-Fashioned Chocolate Chip Cookies

Makes thirty 3-inch cookies

This recipe was handed down by my mother, who is 92 years old and still going strong. Her Toll House cookies are legendary. She undercooked them so they were soft and chewy. I remember loving to eat the batter almost more than the baked cookies. She did everything by hand, with no mixer or food processor.

1 cup (2 sticks) unsalted butter, softened

½ cup granulated sugar

½ cup firmly packed light or dark brown sugar

2 large eggs

1 teaspoon pure vanilla extract

2¼ cups all-purpose flour

1 teaspoon baking soda

¾ teaspoon salt

1 cup semisweet chocolate bits

½ cup coarsely chopped walnuts (optional)

1. Preheat the oven to 375°F. Grease a cookie sheet and set aside.
2. In a large mixing bowl with an electric mixer on high speed (or by hand, using a wooden spoon), cream together the butter and sugars until light and fluffy. Add the eggs one at a time, mixing well after each addition, then add the vanilla. Add the flour, baking soda, and salt and mix until well blended. Stir in the chocolate bits and the walnuts, if using, by hand.
3. Place 1 to 2 tablespoons of cookie dough 2 inches apart in rows on the cookie sheet. Bake until golden brown, 8 to 9 minutes. Remove from the sheet and cool on a wire rack.

ELLEN'S TIPS

★ I underbake for chewy cookies, 7 to 9 minutes, and bake a little longer for crispy cookies, but be careful not to let them burn.

★ Make sure to remove the cookies from the sheet before they cool or they will harden and break when removed.

★ I like small, silver dollar–sized cookies; just don't bake them quite as long.

Bessie's Thumbprint Cookies

Makes thirty 3-inch cookies

My grandmother, Bessie, passed this tradition down to me. I used to watch her when I was 4 years old and my eyes barely cleared the table. My grandchildren love to make these cookies, too, and their thumbs are the perfect size for making the wells for the preserves. It's a good project for a rainy day.

½ cup (1 stick) margarine, softened

¼ cup firmly packed dark brown sugar

1 large egg, separated

½ teaspoon pure vanilla extract

1 cup all-purpose flour

¼ teaspoon salt

12 blanched whole almonds, finely chopped

5 tablespoons fruit preserves of your choice

1. Preheat the oven to 350°F.
2. In a medium-size mixing bowl with an electric mixer on medium speed (or by hand, using a wooden spoon), cream together the margarine and brown sugar until light and fluffy. Add the egg yolk and vanilla and beat for 1 minute.
3. Sift the flour and salt together in a small bowl and add to the batter. Taking ½ teaspoon of dough at a time, roll it into balls.
4. In a small mixing bowl, beat the egg white slightly with a fork. Dip each ball into the beaten egg white and roll in the almonds. Place 1 inch apart on ungreased baking sheets and press your thumb gently into the center of each. Bake until light brown and set, 10 to 12 minutes.
5. Let cool slightly on the sheets, then fill each thumbprint with ½ teaspoon of the preserves and continue cooling on wire racks.

ELLEN'S TIPS

★ Raspberry, strawberry, apricot, and blueberry preserves are my favorites. You can use all of them for variety.

Apricot Ginger Chutney

Makes 2 cups

I first made this chutney in an Indian cooking class about 30 years ago. Sweet and hot at the same time, it adds a wonderful taste dimension to any dish and is particularly great with chops, roasts, chicken, or fish. The real beauty of this chutney is that it keeps in the fridge for 6 months or more. Make sure you always have some on hand.

1 pound dried apricots	1½ cups red wine vinegar
4 cups boiling water	2 cups sugar
One 2-inch piece fresh ginger, peeled	¼ teaspoon salt
	½ teaspoon cayenne pepper
8 large cloves garlic, peeled	¾ cup golden raisins

1. Place the apricots in a large bowl and add the water. Let soak for 2 hours. Drain and cut into quarters.
2. Place the apricots, ginger, garlic, and vinegar in a blender or food processor and process into a paste. Transfer to a large, heavy-bottomed, nonreactive saucepan. Add the sugar, salt, and cayenne and cook over low heat for 35 minutes, stirring often to prevent the sugar from burning. Add the raisins and cook for 10 minutes more.
3. Remove from the heat and let cool. The chutney will thicken as it cools, eventually achieving the consistency of a thick jam. Store in a tightly covered container in the refrigerator. Serve at room temperature.

ELLEN'S TIPS

★ Take care not to burn the chutney while it is cooking. Be vigilant and stir often with a wooden spoon.

★ I keep this chutney on hand to serve with lamb chops or hamburgers. It also goes well with many other dishes, even eggs.

★ At Christmas, I multiply this recipe by 6 for gift giving.

Best Homemade Mustard

Makes 3 cups

ELLEN'S TIPS

★ Cook this in a heavy-bottomed pan, preferably enamel-ware or Teflon-coated. Lower the heat, if necessary, to prevent the sugar from burning.

★ I like to use Colman's dry mustard.

★ Stir the mustard with a wooden spoon, not a metal one, so that you do not loosen any burned pieces that stick to the bottom of the pan. They do not look or taste good in the mustard.

★ I multiply this recipe by 6 at holiday time for gift giving. That makes about 12 to 16 lovely gifts, depending on size.

As with many good recipes, this one has been handed down through the years and has changed gradually in the process. This mustard has become my favorite Christmas gift. I multiply the recipe and put it in pretty apothecary or canning jars decorated with a wide plaid ribbon tied around the top. I always attach the recipe on a 3 x 5-inch card that I've punched a hole in. When we lived in Washington in the early 1980s and my husband, Joe, worked in the White House, I gave the mustard to President Ronald Reagan and Vice President George Bush, and they loved it. One friend used to put it on his scrambled eggs.

One 4-ounce can dry mustard   1 cup cider vinegar
   (see Ellen's Tips)   1 cup sugar
3 large eggs, at room temperature

1. Place the mustard, eggs, vinegar, and sugar in a medium-size, heavy-bottomed, nonreactive saucepan over low heat. Cook, stirring constantly with a wooden spoon, until thickened to the consistency of mayonnaise, about 8 minutes. Don't let the mixture come to a boil.

2. Remove from the heat and let cool to room temperature. Transfer to jars and refrigerate. This will last for at least 6 months.

Berry Crunch Bread

Makes 3 mini loaves or 1 regular loaf

I am not a big bread maker, but this one requires no rising—a big plus, as far as I am concerned. This makes unusually good toast because of its texture—it's really crunchy. It keeps in the refrigerator for six to eight weeks and also freezes well. Wheat berries are small, nutty berries that you can find at health food stores. They give a wonderful crackle to the bread.

One 16-ounce container plain full-fat
    yogurt (see Ellen's Tips)
1 heaping teaspoon baking soda
2 cups whole wheat flour
2 cups wheat germ
1½ tablespoons firmly packed
    dark brown sugar

1½ teaspoons salt
2 tablespoons wheat berries, soaked
    overnight in water to cover
    and drained

1. Preheat the oven to 350°F. Grease 3 mini loaf pans or one 9 x 5-inch loaf pan.
2. In a large mixing bowl, combine the yogurt and baking soda. Add the remaining ingredients and mix well with a fork until everything is evenly distributed. The consistency will seem dry.
3. Spoon the batter into the prepared pan(s) and bake until a skewer inserted in the center comes out clean, about 40 minutes for each mini loaf and 1 hour for the larger loaf. Let cool completely on a wire rack before wrapping in plastic. Store in the refrigerator or freezer (see headnote).

★ Do not use lowfat or nonfat yogurt; both are too watery.

★ If you can't find wheat berries, substitute chopped nuts of your choice.

★ You can buy aluminum foil mini loaf pans in the supermarket.

★ Be careful not to overbake this bread. It is important to keep an eye on your timer.

★ If freezing this bread, it's wise to slice it first so you can toast one slice at a time.

Santa's Coming to Dinner
A Present at Every Place

Little Potato Pancakes with Sour Cream
 and Caviar

Perfect Buttered Noodles

French Three-Meat Stew

Brown Sugar–Baked Acorn Squash

Cranberry Angel Pie

Everyone has his or her own memories and traditions associated with big holidays, and I am no different. Holidays are about making a day special. My father was a pro at this. At our annual Christmas party, held at the old Copley Plaza hotel in Boston, he put a little something wonderful at every place. For the grown-up ladies, he had an orchid corsage—the old-fashioned kind: a big, ruffly white flower with a purple face, stuck with a long hatpin. For the boys he had carnation boutonnieres and for the girls bunches of yellow roses. Each man had a good cigar at his place. And in the center of the table, there was a beautiful music box surrounded by holly or pine boughs.

I like to carry on this tradition at my holiday table by having a gift at each place. It can be something as simple as a bunch of chocolate kisses or horoscope rocks with words that apply to each person: "inspiration," "strength," "perseverance," "whimsy," "love," or whatever seems to fit. Sometimes I put out old photographs as place cards, which the grandchildren think are funny—particularly the ones of their parents. Whatever you do, enjoy planning your own personal touches for these celebrations.

Little Potato Pancakes with Sour Cream and Caviar

Makes 18 pancakes

This can be a lovely side dish, but to kick off a truly special occasion, I like to serve the little pancakes as the hors d'oeuvre or first course. People love their crunch against the smoothness of the sour cream and the briny bite of the caviar.

2 large Idaho potatoes
Pinch of salt and freshly ground
   black pepper
5 tablespoons vegetable oil

5 tablespoons sour cream
4 teaspoons chopped fresh chives
8 ounces sevruga or osetra caviar

1. Peel and shred the potatoes. With your hand, squeeze out all the water onto a paper towel. Transfer to a medium-size mixing bowl, add the salt and pepper, and mix well.
2. Heat the oil in a large nonstick skillet over medium-high heat until very hot but not smoking. Drop a heaping teaspoonful of the shredded potato into the hot oil and, with a metal spatula, press it down into a pancake about 2 inches in diameter. Cook the pancakes, several at a time, until golden brown on the bottom, 2 to 3 minutes. Turn over and brown the other side. Transfer to paper towels to drain. Repeat with the remaining potatoes.
3. Place the pancakes on a warm serving plate and top each with a scant ½ teaspoon sour cream, a pinch of chives, and a scant ½ teaspoon caviar. Serve immediately.

★ Grate on the larger holes, not too fine.

★ Don't try to keep your crispy potato cakes in a warm oven, because they will get soggy. Serve as quickly as possible. If you need to hold them, partially fry them, then fry again right before serving.

★ I serve these on a black lacquer tray with an orchid as decoration.

Perfect Buttered Noodles

Makes 6 to 8 servings

This is one of those not-really-a-recipe recipes. There is no mystery about buttered noodles, but cooking them perfectly can be a bit tricky, as they can turn out too soft or too hard or stick together.

2 quarts water

½ teaspoon salt

1 teaspoon vegetable oil

One and a half 16-ounce packages
   broad egg noodles

5 tablespoons unsalted butter

3 tablespoons chopped fresh parsley
   leaves (optional), for garnish

1. Bring the water to a boil in a large pot over high heat. Add the salt, oil, and noodles, reduce the heat to medium, and stir to mix thoroughly. Cook until soft but not mushy and still slightly chewy, 6 to 8 minutes. Take out a noodle and bite it to check for doneness.

2. Drain in a colander, then transfer to a large, warm serving bowl. Add the butter and toss. Garnish with the parsley, if desired, and serve immediately.

ELLEN'S TIPS

★ Don't let the noodles sit longer than 30 minutes before eating. Even if you keep them warm, buttered, and covered, they tend to stick together soon after cooking.

French Three-Meat Stew

Makes 6 to 8 servings

I learned to make this stew as a young married woman in San Francisco. The unique thing about this recipe is the combination of meats—veal, beef, and lamb. It is a hearty main course, like a hunter's stew, with a good balance of tastes and textures and lots of gravy. Serving it with buttered noodles (page 57) and/or crusty French bread is a must for sopping up the scrumptious sauce.

Seasoned flour:
- 1 cup Wondra flour
- 2 teaspoons garlic salt
- 1 teaspoon dried basil
- 1 teaspoon dried thyme
- 1 teaspoon paprika
- 1 teaspoon freshly ground black pepper

Bouquet garni:
- ½ teaspoon dried basil
- ½ teaspoon dried thyme
- 1 small bay leaf
- 6 black peppercorns

Stew:
- 3 tablespoons butter
- 3 tablespoons canola oil
- 1 pound boneless veal shoulder, trimmed of fat and cut into 1-inch cubes
- 1 pound beef chuck, trimmed of fat and cut into 1-inch cubes
- 1 pound boneless leg of lamb, trimmed of fat and cut into 1-inch cubes
- Salt and freshly ground black pepper to taste
- ¾ cup dry sherry
- 2 cups beef broth, plus more if needed
- 3 medium-size carrots, cut into rough chunks
- 2 cloves garlic, crushed
- 1 large onion, stuck with 2 cloves
- 3 large egg yolks, at room temperature, lightly beaten
- 2 tablespoons fresh lemon juice
- 1 tablespoon heavy cream

1. To make the seasoned flour, combine all the ingredients in a medium-size mixing bowl. Set aside.
2. To make the bouquet garni, wrap all the ingredients in a square of cheesecloth, tie it up like a hobo's pack, and set aside.
3. To make the stew, heat the butter and oil together in a large, heavy skillet over medium-high heat until the butter melts. Sprinkle the meats with salt and pepper, then dredge in the seasoned flour in batches, tapping off any excess flour. Brown on all sides, 1 to 2 minutes per side. Transfer the browned meat to a casserole and set aside. Repeat until all the meat is browned.
4. Pour out most of the oil and butter and deglaze the pan with the sherry and broth over medium heat, scraping the browned bits from the bottom. Add the carrots and garlic and simmer for 1 minute. Transfer to the casserole and add the whole onion. Place the casserole over medium-low heat and cook until the meat is fork tender, 1 to 2 hours, adding more broth or water if needed. Remove the meat and vegetables with a slotted spoon and keep warm.
5. In a medium-size mixing bowl, whisk together the egg yolks, lemon juice, and heavy cream. Add ¼ cup of the warm gravy, whisking constantly. Quickly whisk the egg mixture back into the pan gravy and cook slowly over medium heat until the gravy thickens to the consistency of heavy cream. Return the meat and vegetables to the gravy and warm through. Serve immediately.

ELLEN'S TIPS

★ If you want to thicken the gravy another way, use 2 tablespoons Wondra flour instead of the egg yolk mixture.

★ You can make this stew a day or two ahead.

Brown Sugar-Baked Acorn Squash

Makes 6 to 8 servings

I have always loved squash made this way. We all know that butter and brown sugar make anything taste good.

3 to 4 medium-size to large acorn squash, halved

6 to 8 tablespoons (¾ to 1 stick) butter

6 to 8 tablespoons firmly packed light or dark brown sugar

1. Preheat the oven to 350°F.
2. Scrape out the seeds of the squash with a sharp spoon. Put the squash cut side down in a baking pan. Pour enough water into the pan to go a third of the way up the squash, 2 to 3 cups. Bake until you can pierce the flesh with a sharp knife, 25 to 30 minutes.
3. Take the squash out of the water and place cut side up in a broiling pan. Fill the well of each squash with 1 tablespoon each butter and brown sugar. Broil 1 inch from the heating element until browned and bubbling, about 30 seconds. Serve within 15 minutes.

Cranberry Angel Pie

Makes one 9-inch pie; 8 servings

I got this recipe from my friend James Beard's book on American cooking. The method is simple: make the meringue shell, then the filling, and assemble before serving. Decorate with some whipped cream, and it's ready to eat: light, tart, delicious, and impressive. Don't be put off by meringue; it's really very easy to do.

Pie shell:

1 teaspoon vegetable oil

4 large egg whites, at room temperature

½ teaspoon freshly bought cream of tartar

1 cup sugar

Filling:

4 large egg yolks, at room temperature

½ cup sugar

¼ teaspoon salt

1 cup whole-berry cranberry sauce (canned is fine), pressed through a fine-mesh strainer

1 teaspoon fresh lemon juice

1 cup cold heavy cream

1. To make the pie shell, preheat the oven to 300°F. Grease a 9-inch pie plate lightly with the oil and place it in the oven.

2. In a large mixing bowl with an electric mixer on high speed, beat the egg whites until you get bubbles, then add the cream of tartar. Beat until soft peaks form. Gradually add the sugar and beat until stiff, shiny peaks form. This will take 8 to 9 minutes. Spread the beaten egg whites evenly over the bottom and sides of the warm pie plate. Bake until the shell puffs up and is lightly browned, 40 to 50 minutes.

3. Leave the oven door ajar and let the pie shell cool in the oven for about 30 minutes. The center may sink, and that's okay. Take the shell out of the oven and let cool completely. Set aside.

ELLEN'S TIPS

★ Cream of tartar must be fresh, bought within the past 3 months, to work. Over time, it loses its power to increase the volume of egg whites.

★ Use room temperature egg whites. They give you more volume when beating them, resulting in a better pie shell.

★ The trick to meringue is to beat the egg whites for 8 to 9 minutes, until they really hold a peak. It will seem like a very long time, but it makes a difference for a strong shell.

(continued on page 62)

★ I use a folded potholder to keep the oven door ajar after the shell is baked.

★ The only way to keep the meringue shell crunchy is to assemble the pie just before your guests arrive. I have done it too early, and although it tastes good, the crunchiness is gone.

★ The filling is pale pink and I leave it that way. Some people like to add red food coloring, but not me.

4. To make the filling, in a medium-size stainless steel mixing bowl with an electric mixer on high speed, beat the egg yolks and sugar until light in color, about 3 minutes. Add the salt and strained cranberry sauce. Stir in the lemon juice. Use a double boiler or place the bowl over a large saucepan with about 2 inches of boiling water and stir, making sure the bowl is not touching the water, until the custard thickens. The consistency should be like that of mayonnaise. (It will thicken more when chilled.) Cover with plastic wrap and refrigerate for at least 1 hour or overnight.

5. At least 2 hours before serving, take the custard out of the refrigerator. When it comes to room temperature, beat with a fork to loosen it.

6. About 30 minutes before serving, beat the heavy cream in a medium-size bowl with an electric mixer on high speed until stiff peaks form.

7. Assemble the pie as close to serving time as possible. If the pie shell hasn't fallen on its own, crack it to make a well. Spread the custard filling in the shell, then spread the whipped cream evenly over the top, or decorate with a pastry bag. Serve immediately.

Hurry Up and Eat Breakfast

Before Running to See Three Movies

Joe's Scrambies

Our Famous Cinnamon Toast

My husband and I like to catch up on movies three at a time. The intense scheduling with the newspaper over breakfast, pencil and paper in hand, is quite something to witness. We usually end up seeing one choice of his, one of mine, and one compromise. And to make sure we don't eat only Raisinets and buttered popcorn all day, Joe cooks his famous "scrambies" and cinnamon toast while I read the schedules and theater locations out loud. Our personal best was four films in one day, although I don't recommend that program for a clear night's sleep.

Joe's Scrambies

Makes 2 to 4 servings

I learned this way of making scrambled eggs from my good-cook husband, Joe. It's all in the method of scrambling slowly with a spoon.

2 tablespoons butter

4 to 5 large eggs

1 slice Velveeta cheese, broken
  into small pieces

Salt and freshly ground black
  pepper to taste

Optional additions:

  2 teaspoons chopped fresh chives or
    scallions (white and green parts)

  ½ teaspoon Dijon mustard

  1 teaspoon chopped fresh
    parsley leaves

  Tabasco sauce to taste

Heat the butter in a medium-size skillet over medium heat until it is melted. Reduce the heat to low, break the eggs into the pan, and mix slowly with a spoon until they begin to scramble. Add the cheese and keep mixing slowly. Add any of the optional additions and cook soft, hard, or in between. Sprinkle with salt and pepper and serve immediately.

ELLEN'S TIPS

★ I like my eggs fairly simple and clean. Joe, on the other hand, likes his very seasoned, so you may choose your own way of doing these "scrambies."

Our Famous
Cinnamon Toast

Makes 1 toast

This is simply the best cinnamon toast, another wonderful no-recipe recipe from my husband, Joe. I like to use Pepperidge Farm bread.

1 slice white bread
1 tablespoon butter, softened

2 teaspoons cinnamon sugar
(see Ellen's Tips)

Spread one side of the bread with the butter and sprinkle on the cinnamon sugar. Toast in a toaster oven until the sugar bubbles and is caramelized, about 3 minutes. As it cools, it gets crispy and delicious.

Under the Weather

Almost Makes It Worth Having a Cold

The Wright Pea Soup

Palacinki

Cold milk or hot tea

Not that I like getting sick, but when it does happen, my husband makes me his favorite dish from childhood, palacinki—thin crepes filled with cream cheese and jam, rolled up and topped with browned butter and sifted confectioners' sugar. Joe says I could eat browned butter and powdered sugar on a burned cork. He's right. Joe's recipe came from his mother, Anne Cech, who moved to the United States from Czechoslovakia when she was 11. Every nationality has their version of these crepes. In my case, it was my Russian grandmother, Bessie, who made blintzes. My favorite filling is apricot jam, but I have gobbled up many a palacinki made with strawberry, cherry, or peach jam, among other flavors. Somehow, it all tastes better when brought to you on a tray.

The Wright Pea Soup

Makes 8 to 10 servings

This is another family heirloom recipe from my Czechoslovakian mother-in-law, Anne Cech. She was a very good cook and someone I respected for her instinctive culinary sense. Common sense is something you can't teach, and she had it. I love to make this soup when it's cold outside. It travels especially well if you are going away for the weekend and want to bring something. We love eating this soup with black bread and sweet butter.

1 meaty ham bone

3 chicken bouillon cubes

One 16-ounce package dried split peas, yellow or green, rinsed and picked over

2 medium-size onions, finely chopped

2 medium-size potatoes (preferably russet or Yukon Gold), peeled and finely diced

2 medium-size carrots, diced (2 cups)

2 ribs celery, diced (1 cup)

1 clove garlic, crushed and chopped

1 bay leaf

1 teaspoon sugar

2 teaspoons fresh lemon juice

Freshly ground black pepper to taste

Croutons:

8 medium-thick slices bread (see Ellen's Tips)

6 tablespoons (¾ stick) butter

2 tablespoons canola oil

Roux:

2 tablespoons butter

2 tablespoons all-purpose flour

2 tablespoons finely chopped scallion greens, for garnish

2 tablespoons chopped fresh parsley leaves, for garnish

ELLEN'S TIPS

★ Stir the soup with a wooden spoon from time to time to keep it from sticking to the bottom of the pot.

★ This recipe needs no salt because the ham bone has enough. You must always taste soup before you season it.

★ You do not need to soak the peas overnight. In the old days, the purpose of soaking overnight was to soften the peas and reduce the cooking time.

★ I like to use 7-grain bread for the croutons, but you may also use Italian, French, or sourdough.

(continued on page 70)

ELLEN'S TIPS

(continued from page 69)

★ My mother-in-law insisted that her pea soup tasted so good because of the roux. She was right.

★ You can prepare this soup a day or two ahead and reheat. It also will hold in the freezer for at least 1 month. To avoid freezer burn, place the soup in a plastic container; wrap in plastic, then aluminum foil, and cover. Defrost, then reheat with a bit of water if necessary.

★ To make a more substantial meal, serve the soup with grilled knockwurst and hot mustard.

1. Place the ham bone, bouillon cubes, split peas, and onions in a large stockpot with cold water to cover. Bring to a boil over high heat, then reduce the heat to medium-low and simmer, uncovered, for 1½ hours. Transfer the ham bone to a plate and set aside. When cool enough to handle, tear the meat off the bone into bite-size pieces.

2. Add the potatoes, carrots, celery, garlic, bay leaf, sugar, lemon juice, and pepper to the pot. Return the ham bone and shredded meat and simmer, covered, over low heat until the peas have broken down and the vegetables are very soft, about 2 hours. Discard the bone.

3. Meanwhile, if using, make the croutons. Remove the crusts from the bread and cut into 1-inch cubes. In a large skillet over medium-high heat, heat the butter and oil together until the butter bubbles. Brown the bread cubes on all sides, shaking the pan as you go. Transfer to paper towels to drain.

4. To make the roux, place the butter in a small skillet over low heat. Add the flour and stir until browned, about 2 minutes. Add a ladleful of the soup to the roux and stir until the mixture is smooth. Stir this back into the soup to thicken.

5. As soon as the soup has thickened, ladle it into bowls, garnish with the scallions or parsley, and top with the croutons.

Palacinki

Makes about 10 crepes

When I am not feeling well, Joe, my sweet husband, serves these to me, and I swear they make me feel better. I know that sounds crazy, but these crepes are so good they must have healing powers. The combination of cream cheese and preserves inside with the browned butter and confectioners' sugar outside is unbeatable. It is the chicken soup of desserts.

2 cups all-purpose flour
1 cup whole milk
½ to 1 cup water, as needed
4 large eggs
Pinch of salt
One 8-ounce package cream cheese, softened

¼ cup (½ stick) unsalted butter
About ¾ cup fruit preserves of your choice
1 cup confectioners' sugar
½ cup (1 stick) unsalted butter, melted over low heat and cooked until just browned (don't let it burn)

1. Place the flour and milk in a blender and process until smooth. Add ½ cup of the water, the eggs, and salt and process again until smooth. Add more water if necessary to achieve the consistency of heavy cream.

2. In a crepe pan or flat skillet over medium heat, melt 1 teaspoon of the butter until it bubbles. Distribute the butter all over the bottom and up the sides of the pan. Pour in a few small ladlefuls of batter and tilt the pan until the batter covers the bottom. When the crepe is done on one side only, about 1 minute, lift it out of the pan with a metal spatula and transfer to a warm plate. Cover each crepe with a sheet of waxed paper and continue the process, stacking the crepes on the plate, until all the batter is used.

3. To assemble the crepes, spread each crepe with about 1 tablespoon of the softened cream cheese, leaving a 1-inch border. Spread 2 teaspoons of the preserves on the cream cheese and roll up. Place on a plate and continue with the remaining crepes.

4. When all of the crepes have been filled, sift the confectioners' sugar generously over the tops, drizzle the browned butter over them, and serve immediately.

ELLEN'S TIPS

★ Instead of preserves, you can put cinnamon sugar on the cream cheese, if you like.

★ This recipe may yield more crepes than you want to use. If so, wrap them separately in plastic and then aluminum foil, stack, and freeze. Defrost at room temperature and fill as desired.

Time for Resolutions

New Year's Eve at the Wrights'

Galette with Gorgonzola and Cherry Tomatoes

Pam's Beef Tenderloin with Horseradish Sauce

Marjoram Onions

Boston Lettuce with Asian Dressing

Crispy Baked Potatoes with Caviar

Crunchy Pecan Pie

My horoscope says that because I am a Capricorn, I am a homebody. But I know many friends whose birthdays fall elsewhere in the calendar who agree with me—there is no night of the year I like to stay home more than New Year's Eve. I love to be with close friends and family on this very special night. I light every candle in the house to create a mood of warmth and celebration. Music is also a must. We each write our resolutions on a piece of paper, seal them inside an envelope, and give them to someone else to keep until next year. Then we open last year's resolutions and see how we did. It's always a surprise and makes for good conversation.

As for the meal, I could be happy eating caviar and baked potatoes for my whole dinner, along with a glass of champagne, but I realize others might want something a bit more substantial. You can still keep it simple, though, and add some flair with a few dressy touches such as silver candlesticks, crystal glasses, and your best napkins.

I serve this meal in sections. When the guests arrive and have a glass of champagne in hand, I serve the galette. I have a knife and server next to it, along with a stack of plates, so that people can help themselves. The rest of the meal is served buffet style on a sideboard so that guests can take what they like. After all, New Year's Eve is a night to enjoy.

Galette with Gorgonzola and Cherry Tomatoes

Makes 6 servings

This pie makes a fabulous hors d'oeuvre or lunch dish. The dough requires yeast, and that usually scares people. But it's easy to do and can be prepared ahead and then frozen or refrigerated until you're ready to use it. This dish looks so yummy with the melted cheese studded with bright red tomatoes peeking out of the center of the homemade pastry.

Dough:

1 package active dry yeast
   (check the expiration date)
½ cup warm water (about 110°F;
   see Ellen's Tips)
½ teaspoon sugar
1½ cups all-purpose flour
½ teaspoon salt
3 tablespoons unsalted butter,
   softened

Filling:

3 tablespoons unsalted butter
2½ pounds onions, thinly sliced

3 ounces Gorgonzola cheese, crumbled
8 cherry tomatoes, halved
2 teaspoons chopped fresh thyme
   leaves or 1 teaspoon dried
Salt and freshly ground black pepper
   to taste
3 tablespoons olive oil
1 large egg, beaten

2 to 3 sprigs fresh thyme, for garnish
Cherry tomatoes, on the vine, for
   garnish

ELLEN'S TIPS

★ If the water you use to make the dough is too cold, it won't activate the yeast; if it's too hot, it will kill the yeast. The temperature of the water should be about 110°F. If you don't have a thermometer, use my "finger test." Dip your pinkie into the water; if you don't feel anything—not cold, cool, or hot— it is just the right temperature.

★ Dough brushed with beaten egg takes on a nice shine when baked.

(continued on page 76)

1. To make the dough, in a small bowl, dissolve the yeast in the water. Add the sugar and stir. Let sit for about 5 minutes. If it bubbles, the yeast is active.

2. Put the yeast-water mixture, flour, and salt in a medium-size mixing bowl and mix with a wooden spoon or an electric mixer fitted with a dough hook until the dough comes together. If mixing by hand, transfer the dough to a lightly floured work surface and knead until the dough is elastic and stiff; if using a standing mixer, this will take 5 to 10 minutes. Grease a medium-size bowl with the butter, place the

Crispy Baked Potatoes with Caviar

Makes 6 servings

Serve these for a tailor-made baked potato night. I like to use a mother-of-pearl or wooden spoon for the caviar and little condiment bowls for the sour cream and onions. The fun part is designing your own.

6 medium-size baking potatoes
  (preferably Idaho)
2 tablespoons olive oil
Kosher salt to taste

12 ounces osetra caviar
2 cups sour cream
½ cup chopped fresh chives or
  finely chopped onion

1. Preheat the oven to 400°F.
2. Wash and dry the potatoes. Pierce each potato with a sharp knife or fork in 3 or 4 places. Rub with the olive oil and sprinkle with salt.
3. Bake until the skin is crispy and the center is tender when tested with a fork, 40 to 45 minutes.
4. Place the caviar, sour cream, and chives in separate bowls and let guests add them (or not) to their baked potatoes.
5. Serve with additional condiments in individual bowls, such as crumbled blue cheese, finely chopped scallion greens, and crumbled crisp bacon.

ELLEN'S TIPS

★ If you are baking more than 6 potatoes, allow more time for baking, as the heat doesn't circulate as effectively in the oven when there are that many items.

★ I like sevruga and beluga caviar, too. American caviar is also an option. Which you choose is a matter of taste and budget.

Crunchy Pecan Pie

Makes one 9-inch pie; 8 servings

★ To make rolling the dough easier, flour your rolling pin as well as your work surface. Don't be afraid to gently pick up the dough and turn it to prevent it from sticking.

★ To transfer the dough to the pie plate, loosely roll it around the rolling pin and unroll it over the pie plate. This helps keep the dough from tearing.

★ It is necessary to make the edge of the crust taller than the pie plate because most pastry shrinks as it bakes.

I learned to make this pie because I used to get pecans every Christmas from our dear friends from Atlanta, the Elsons. Every year, I tried another pecan recipe, and this one is my favorite. I love these buttery chopped nuts, which rise to the top and brown so nicely. Serve plain or with whipped cream or ice cream.

2 large eggs, at room temperature
1 cup dark corn syrup
¾ cup firmly packed dark
   brown sugar
1 teaspoon pure vanilla extract
1 tablespoon dark rum

¼ teaspoon salt
1 recipe Foolproof Piecrust
   (recipe follows)
1 cup coarsely chopped pecans
2 tablespoons unsalted butter,
   cut into small pieces

1. Preheat the oven to 450°F.
2. In a large mixing bowl with an electric mixer on low speed, beat the eggs, corn syrup, brown sugar, vanilla, rum, and salt until combined. Set aside.
3. On a lightly floured work surface, roll out the piecrust to ¼ inch thick. Carefully transfer it to a 9-inch pie plate and fit into the bottom and sides. Trim the excess dough, leaving enough so that it stands about ¼ inch above the edge of the plate. Then crimp the edge of the crust, using the knuckles of one hand on the inside while pinching the dough with the other to form a fluted edge.
4. Sprinkle the pecans evenly over the crust. Pour in the filling and dot with the butter.
5. Bake on the center oven rack for 10 minutes. Reduce the oven temperature to 325°F and bake until the filling sets, 25 to 30 minutes. Let cool completely before serving.

Foolproof Piecrust

Makes enough for 1 single-crust 9-inch pie

This recipe is an oldie but a goodie. I have been making it since 1959, when I was going to summer school in Berkeley, California, and my neighbor Ursula taught it to me. It was as easy as she said, and the side benefit was my discovery of piecrust cookies (see page 45).

1¼ cups all-purpose flour

1 teaspoon baking powder

2 tablespoons sugar

Pinch of salt

½ cup vegetable shortening

¼ cup whole milk

In a large mixing bowl, sift together the flour, baking powder, sugar, and salt. Add the shortening and work it in using a pastry cutter or your fingertips until it looks like coarse meal. Add the milk, little by little, mixing until the dough comes together in a ball. Cover with plastic wrap and refrigerate until ready to use.

ELLEN'S TIPS

★ If you wish to make a good pie shell, roll the dough out to about ¼ inch thick and do not overhandle it.

★ You can refrigerate the unbaked pie shell, well covered with plastic wrap, overnight.

Boys in One Room, Girls in Another

Super Bowl Supper

Margarita Contest

Stuffed Mushrooms with Shallots

Chunky Guacamole with Tortilla Chips
   and Endive Spears

Spicy Chicken Nuggets with Blue Cheese Dip

Oklahoma Chili

Key Lime Squares

Any festivity that starts off with a pitcher of margaritas has a good chance of success. The competition for best margarita is fierce in my household. My children and their friends all fight hard for first place. No matter who wins, the drinks are fun to serve, especially when the chili is hot and the cheering for your team gets loud.

It always seems that at an event like this, the men end up in one room and the women in another. In some houses, the ladies gather in the kitchen; in my house, it's the bathroom. My bathroom is a bit unusual: it is bigger than my bedroom. It has large windows that overlook a small playground and the East River. Not that we look at the view too long, because we are too busy doing girl things, drinking margaritas, trying on clothes, and just chatting away. When dinner is ready, we reluctantly come out to get our plates and go right back in to our comfy privacy.

Margarita Contest

I used to think that margaritas were really hard to make and that the only good place to have them was at a Mexican restaurant. I was wrong. I have since learned several competing recipes. I include three here for your perusal. One comes from a retired heart surgeon, Bob. One is from Geoff, a friend of my son's, who is in his thirties and works in the record business. The other is from my older daughter, Claudia, a mother of three.

Bob's Margaritas
Makes 8 to 10 drinks

1 cup ice
One and a half 8-ounce cans frozen
    limeade concentrate

4 cups tequila
½ cup Triple Sec

Put all the ingredients in a blender and blend at high speed until slushy.

Geoff's "Kick-Ass Margs"
Makes 8 to 10 drinks

A pitcher of ice
4 cups Sauza Gold or Hornitos tequila

2 cups Cointreau
1 cup fresh lime juice

Combine all the ingredients in a blender, then buckle your seat belts.

Claudia's Margaritas
Makes 8 to 10 drinks

A pitcher of ice
1 cup fresh orange juice
1 cup fresh lime juice

1 cup Triple Sec
3 cups tequila

Combine all the ingredients in a blender.

Stuffed Mushrooms
with Shallots

Makes 6 to 8 servings

I made this recipe up one weekend when I was having people for cocktails. These mushrooms are so easy to make and taste wonderful. For your Super Bowl party, you can assemble them in the morning and bake just before serving. Or you can make them ahead and keep them in the freezer for future parties.

2 tablespoons butter

1 teaspoon canola oil

3 large shallots, finely chopped

12 to 16 small mushrooms, stems
    finely chopped and caps set aside

½ teaspoon Worcestershire sauce

2 tablespoons plain dry
    bread crumbs

1. Preheat the oven to 375°F.
2. In a medium-size skillet over medium heat, heat the butter and oil together until the butter is bubbling. Add the shallots and cook, stirring, until transparent, about 4 minutes. Add the chopped mushroom stems and cook, stirring constantly, until browned, about 3 minutes. Remove from the heat, add the Worcestershire and bread crumbs, and mix with a fork.
3. Stuff each mushroom cap with a teaspoon of the shallot mixture and place the caps in a baking pan. You can cover and refrigerate until ready to bake, if you wish.
4. Bake the mushrooms until heated through, about 6 minutes, and serve immediately.

ELLEN'S TIPS

★ Do not wash mushrooms. Instead, wipe them with a paper towel to clean.

★ Choose mushrooms that are bite size. Don't make the mistake of getting huge ones, which are hard to eat.

★ You can add 1 tablespoon chopped fresh parsley leaves, cilantro leaves, or chives to the stuffing mixture, if you wish.

Chunky Guacamole with Tortilla Chips and Endive Spears

Makes 6 to 8 servings

ELLEN'S TIPS

★ You can keep guacamole without browning for up to 2 days if you keep the pit in the mixture and wrap well.

★ Instead of tortilla chips, I sometimes use toasted bagel chips, crackers, or Homemade Tortilla Chips (page 187).

Nothing is better than fresh avocados chopped into a chunky guacamole, rather than the usual smooth dip. I don't like a complicated guacamole, so this has only tomato, onion, and seasonings in it. It can be made in the morning and served that evening if you use the pit trick: push an avocado pit into the mash, and it won't turn brown.

2 ripe avocados (preferably Hass), peeled and pitted (reserve 1 pit)
1 medium-size ripe tomato, cored and cut into 1-inch pieces
1 small red onion, cut into 1-inch pieces
1 tablespoon fresh lemon juice

Dash of Tabasco sauce
Salt and freshly ground black pepper to taste
Tortilla chips
1 Belgian endive, separated into individual spears

1. Cut the avocados coarsely into a medium-size mixing bowl and mash slightly. Add the tomato and onion, then the lemon juice and Tabasco. Season with salt and pepper. Mix the guacamole with a fork and push the reserved pit into the mixture. Cover tightly with plastic wrap and refrigerate until serving.
2. Serve with tortilla chips and the endive spears.

Spicy Chicken Nuggets with Blue Cheese Dip

Makes 6 to 8 servings

When cut into small pieces, the chicken cooks up tasty and crispy and is very handy to eat. Big kids and little kids all love these.

Blue cheese dip:
- 1 cup plain yogurt
- ¼ cup mashed blue cheese

Seasoned flour:
- 2 cups Wondra flour
- 2 teaspoons garlic salt
- 1 teaspoon dried basil
- 1 teaspoon dried oregano

- 1 teaspoon paprika
- ½ teaspoon freshly ground black pepper

- 3 boneless, skinless chicken breast halves
- 2 cups canola oil
- Kosher salt to taste

1. To make the dip, combine the yogurt and blue cheese in a small bowl, mixing well with a fork until smooth. Cover and refrigerate until ready to use.
2. To make the seasoned flour, combine all the ingredients in a shallow bowl.
3. Cut the chicken into 1½- to 2-inch-long pieces and dredge them in the seasoned flour, tapping off any excess.
4. In a large skillet over medium-high heat, heat the oil until hot but not smoking. Drop the floured chicken pieces into the oil in batches (be careful not to crowd them, or they won't fry up crisp) and cook until nicely browned on both sides, about 5 minutes. Transfer to a plate lined with paper towels to drain. Continue until all the chicken is cooked.
5. Sprinkle with salt and serve warm with the dip on the side.

Oklahoma Chili

Makes 6 to 8 servings

My husband is an Okie, born and bred in Tulsa. Some of his closest relatives have strong opinions about chili, especially that it doesn't include beans. To do so is almost a crime. Joe likes it spicy, with chopped onion on the side. I like it milder, with the onion added in. You can garnish the chili with more chopped onion, grated cheddar cheese, sour cream, and/or jalapeño chile peppers.

3 pounds ground chuck
1 tablespoon canola oil
1 large onion, chopped
2 tablespoons chili powder
1 teaspoon ground cumin
2 teaspoons paprika
½ teaspoon cayenne pepper, or to taste
Two 4-ounce cans tomato sauce
3 cups water
¼ cup masa harina or yellow cornmeal

Garnish:

1 medium-size onion, chopped
1 cup shredded cheddar cheese
1 cup sour cream
2 or 3 jalapeño chile peppers, chopped

Twelve 6-inch soft corn tortillas,
  brushed with a bit of butter,
  wrapped in aluminum foil, and
  warmed in a 350°F oven

1. In a large skillet over medium-high heat, brown the ground chuck until it is no longer pink, breaking it up as you cook. Drain the fat out of the pan.
2. In a medium-size skillet over medium heat, heat the canola oil. Add the onion and cook, stirring, until softened. Add the onion to the meat, along with the chili powder, cumin, paprika, and cayenne, and stir. Add the tomato sauce and water and mix well. Reduce the heat to a simmer and cook, covered, for 30 minutes.
3. Stir in the masa harina and cook over low heat for about 5 minutes. Keep warm.
4. Serve the chili in individual bowls with the chopped onion, grated cheese, sour cream, and jalapeños in separate bowls as condiments. Serve the warm tortillas in a basket lined with a clean dishtowel or pretty napkin.

ELLEN'S TIPS

★ In place of tortillas, serve a basket of your favorite large tortilla chips.

★ Serve with white rice on the side.

★ Add I cup drained canned kidney beans if you are a bean lover.

★ Serve with your favorite salsa or Tabasco sauce for those who need that extra zip.

★ Masa harina is Spanish ground cornmeal flour.

Key Lime Squares

Makes about twenty 2-inch squares

I acquired the recipe for this terrific tart in Florida while living in a house at the beach. It is a dessert you can bring to your neighbor's house for a gift because it travels well and is a refreshing end to any dinner. You can buy bottled Key lime juice, which tastes quite good.

5 large eggs, at room temperature

2 cups granulated sugar

¾ cup Key lime juice

1 cup (2 sticks) unsalted butter

3 ounces blanched almonds, finely chopped

2¼ cups all-purpose flour

1 tablespoon plus ¼ cup confectioners' sugar

1. Preheat the oven to 350°F.
2. In a medium-size mixing bowl with an electric mixer on medium speed, beat the eggs, granulated sugar, and lime juice until foamy, 3 to 4 minutes. Set aside.
3. In another medium-size mixing bowl, mash the butter with a fork. Add the almonds, flour, and 1 tablespoon of the confectioners' sugar to form a dough. Pat the dough into the bottom of a 9 x 13-inch baking dish.
4. Bake the crust on the center oven rack for 15 minutes. Remove from the oven and reduce the temperature to 325°F. Pour the filling into the crust and bake until set, 20 to 30 minutes. If the squares do not set in 30 minutes, turn off the oven and leave the pan inside with the door ajar until they are firm. Remove from the oven and let cool completely.
5. Sift the remaining ¼ cup confectioners' sugar evenly over the top just before serving.

ELLEN'S TIPS

★ You can substitute fresh lemon juice if you can't find bottled Key lime juice (regular bottled lime juice just isn't right in this recipe).

★ These taste best fresh. You can refrigerate them, but the crust will get soft.

Six and the City
Valentine Candlelight Dinner

Garlic-Crumb Broiled Tomatoes

Baked Bacon Bread Sticks

Sweet Potato Cottage Fries

Two-White/Two-Green Salmon

Frances's Peach Cake

In New York City, the two most difficult nights to get a reservation in a restaurant are New Year's Eve and Valentine's Day. The two holidays are similar in that there are high expectations on both. Instead of having the usual romantic dinner alone, I have a Valentine's Day party with two other couples, preferably ones who really like each other. It's a good excuse to decorate the table with everything from old-fashioned paper doilies to cinnamon hearts in tiny bowls. You can be sophisticated in your décor, whimsical, or downright romantic with hearts and flowers. Try your hand at being creative. The meal is light and tasty, ending with the peach upside-down cake. And because they didn't have to fight the crowds of lovers dining out, your guests will depart with smiles on their faces and love in their hearts.

Garlic-Crumb Broiled Tomatoes

Makes 6 servings

These halved tomatoes are broiled with bread crumbs, parsley, and garlic. They are a good addition to any meal but great with a soufflé, a chop or burger, or even a grilled cheese sandwich.

¼ cup extra virgin olive oil

¼ cup chopped fresh parsley leaves

4 to 5 large cloves garlic, to your taste, finely chopped

3 large ripe tomatoes

Salt and freshly ground black pepper to taste

4 teaspoons plain dry bread crumbs

1. In a small mixing bowl, combine the olive oil, parsley, and garlic.
2. Wash and dry the tomatoes. Remove the stem ends by making a shallow well in the center. Place cut side up in a broiling pan. Drizzle with the olive oil mixture and season with salt and pepper. Sprinkle the tops evenly with the bread crumbs, pressing some extra filling into the center.
3. Broil until browned, 1 to 2 minutes. Serve immediately.

ELLEN'S TIPS

★ You can use herbed bread crumbs, but leave out the parsley.

★ You can substitute other herbs for the parsley. Rosemary, thyme, sage, and basil all work nicely, but don't use more than 2 or 3.

★ Don't leave the oven when broiling. It takes only a second for the tomatoes to burn.

Baked Bacon Bread Sticks

Makes 18 bread sticks

ELLEN'S TIPS

★ If you'll be serving only grownups, try substituting ¼ cup bourbon for the Worcestershire.

★ Try not to use bacon that is too lean, or it won't adhere to the sticks.

One weekend I was testing this recipe, and before I knew it, I had eaten almost the entire batch. They are that good and impossible to resist.
Serve right out of the oven.

18 crisp breadsticks

18 strips thinly sliced bacon

½ cup firmly packed dark brown sugar

2 tablespoons Worcestershire sauce

1. Preheat the oven to 300°F.
2. Wrap each bread stick with a bacon strip. Sprinkle with brown sugar and a few drops of Worcestershire.
3. Place the bread sticks on a wire rack set over a baking sheet and bake until browned and crispy, 10 to 15 minutes.

Sweet Potato Cottage Fries

Makes 6 servings

ELLEN'S TIPS

★ These fries will get soggy if kept in the oven for more than 10 minutes. Try to serve them as soon as possible.

I had the pleasure of eating these in Florida many years ago, and I decided to make them at home. They are easy to prepare and a nice change from regular white potatoes.

2 cups canola oil

3 large sweet potatoes, peeled
   and thinly sliced

Sea salt or kosher salt
   to taste

In a large, heavy skillet over medium-high heat, heat the canola oil. When it is very hot but not smoking, carefully drop in the sweet potatoes in batches, taking care not to crowd them. Cook until golden brown on both sides, about 4 minutes total. Using a slotted spoon, transfer to paper towels to drain. Keep warm in a low oven as you fry the remaining batches. Sprinkle with salt before serving

Two-White / Two-Green Salmon

Makes 6 servings

My daughter Claudia gave me this recipe. She lives with her three small children in Washington, D.C., and she entertains often. She likes recipes that are easy but satisfying. This salmon, spread with a paste made of two white and two green ingredients, is terrific and very tasty.

6 salmon fillets (about ½ pound each)

6 tablespoons mayonnaise

¼ cup freshly grated Parmesan cheese

¼ cup chopped fresh dill

¼ cup chopped scallion greens

1. Preheat the oven to 350°F.
2. Rinse the salmon fillets with cold water and dry with paper towels. Place in a single layer in a lightly buttered baking dish.
3. Place the mayonnaise, Parmesan, dill, and scallions in a food processor and pulse until processed into a smooth paste. Spread the paste generously on the salmon fillets.
4. Bake until the fish flakes with a fork, 30 to 40 minutes. Serve hot.

ELLEN'S TIPS

★ You can prepare the salmon for the oven in the morning, spreading the fillets with the paste, then covering with plastic wrap. Keep in the refrigerator until ½ hour before baking.

★ Of course, you can use this topping on any fish. I have also tried it on swordfish, flounder, and orange roughy.

Frances's Peach Cake

Makes 6 to 8 servings

This cake is from a mystery woman named Frances, whom I never met. The recipe was handed around in San Francisco when I was first married in 1960. I can't remember how it got to me, but I have been making it all these years. This is one of the most delicate butter cakes I've ever eaten. It's made with canned peaches, which are lifesavers when fresh peaches are not available.

½ cup (1 stick) unsalted butter

1 cup granulated sugar

2 large eggs

1½ cups all-purpose flour

1½ teaspoons baking powder

Pinch of salt

About 6 large canned peach halves
   (see Ellen's Tips)

½ teaspoon ground cinnamon

1 tablespoon light or dark
   brown sugar

2 teaspoons fresh lemon juice

1 cup heavy cream, whipped to
   stiff peaks, or vanilla ice cream,
   for serving

1. Preheat the oven to 350°F. Butter and flour an 8-inch square pan and knock out the excess flour.
2. In a medium-size mixing bowl using an electric mixer on medium-high speed, beat the butter and granulated sugar until the mixture is pale yellow. Add the eggs, flour, baking powder, and salt and continue to beat for 5 minutes.
3. Place the peach halves cut side down in the prepared pan and sprinkle with the cinnamon, brown sugar, and lemon juice. Spoon in the batter and bake on the center oven rack until a cake tester inserted in the center comes out clean, 40 to 45 minutes.
4. Remove the pan from the oven and let cool slightly. Unmold the cake on a pretty plate (see Ellen's Tips). Serve warm with the whipped cream.

★ Canned peaches vary greatly in size, so you may need fewer or more.

★ Cut the peaches into hearts for Valentine's Day.

★ You may use fresh peaches for this recipe, but make sure they are perfect.

★ To unmold the cake, run a sharp knife carefully around the edges. Don't be scared if it doesn't work the first time or if the entire cake doesn't come out in one gorgeous piece. You can piece it together yourself.

★ I like to serve this cake slightly warm.

Freezing Cold Winter Night

Come Sit by the Fire

Tiny French Radish Sandwiches

Piroshkies

Brisket and Cabbage Soup

Mixed green salad with one of Ellen's
   Favorite Dressings

Warm Apple Crisp with Homemade
   Vanilla Ice Cream

Perfect for a Sunday night or a school night, a supper like this makes you think you should eat it in your kitchen, wearing jeans and a big warm sweater or, better yet, your favorite sweats. But sometimes I like to do the opposite. I have served this menu on my good china, in fancy bowls, with silver and crystal. When you have a dinner party, it's important not to get beaten down by the pressure of serving a standing rib roast of beef or a leg of lamb. It takes courage to serve something "homey" like a thick soup with salad and bread. I know it is much appreciated. I use large, low Chinese bowls for the soup. Put your *piroshkies*, which are little meat-filled dumplings, in a basket lined with a beautiful napkin to keep them warm. Instead of giant balloon wineglasses, I like to use small juice glasses for wine. Everyone will feel the warmth of your home, and not just from the fireplace—from the kind of meal, the relaxed feeling, and the sense of well-being you offer.

Tiny French Radish Sandwiches

Makes 12 hors d'oeuvres

My French daughter-in-law, Celine, always has such elegance in her simplicity, and these remind me of her style. They are literally radish sandwiches, made with French bread, butter, and salt. I have shrunk them down to hors d'oeuvre size for this meal. The crunch is perfect for the occasion.

¼ cup (½ stick) butter, softened
½ French baguette, cut into 12 slices
   (about ½ inch thick)
12 radishes, trimmed and sliced

Kosher salt to taste
1 perfect bunch radishes, with the
   greens left on, for garnish

Butter one side of each bread slice and top with radish slices. Press the radishes into the butter and sprinkle with salt. Serve the little slices like bruschetta, on a pretty platter garnished with the whole bunch of radishes on one side.

Piroshkies

Makes 18 to 24 dumplings

These baked meat dumplings go very well with soups or salads, especially thick, hearty soups like this one. Served alone, they make a nice hors d'oeuvre. Or pair them with a salad and serve for lunch. I like them because they can be made ahead and frozen for any of those occasions.

Dough:

3⅓ cups all-purpose flour

1 teaspoon baking powder

1 teaspoon salt

1 teaspoon sugar

½ cup vegetable shortening

2 large eggs, at room temperature,
  lightly beaten

1 cup sour cream

Filling:

¼ cup (½ stick) butter

2 medium-size onions, finely chopped

1 pound lean ground beef

2 tablespoons chopped fresh dill

Salt and freshly ground black
  pepper to taste

1 tablespoon all-purpose flour

2 tablespoons water

1 large egg, at room temperature,
  beaten with 2 teaspoons cold water

1. To make the dough, sift the flour, baking powder, salt, and sugar in a medium-size bowl twice. Place in a food processor and add the shortening. Pulse until the mixture resembles coarse meal. Add the eggs and sour cream and pulse lightly until the dough gathers into a ball. Remove from the processor and wrap in plastic. Refrigerate for at least 1 hour.

2. To make the filling, heat 2 tablespoons of the butter in a medium-size skillet over medium heat. Add the onions and cook, stirring, until lightly browned, 2 to 3 minutes. Add the remaining 2 tablespoons butter and the ground beef. Cook, breaking it up, until lightly browned all over, about 5 minutes. Add the dill and season with salt and pepper. Using a slotted spoon, transfer the meat mixture to a plate.

ELLEN'S TIPS

★ You can refrigerate the dough and filling overnight, in separate dishes. The dumplings can be assembled the next day.

★ These dumplings freeze very well after they are baked. Wrap tightly in plastic and freeze in an airtight tin. Do not defrost them; just pop them directly in a 400°F oven and bake until golden brown, 12 to 15 minutes.

★ You can use 2 circles of dough to make bigger dumplings, if you wish.

3. In the same skillet over low heat, brown the flour in the leftover butter and fat. Add the water and stir until thickened, scraping the browned bits from the bottom of the pan. Return the meat to the pan and coat with the sauce. Remove from the heat and set aside until you are ready to make the dumplings.

4. Preheat the oven to 425°F.

5. Roll out the dough as thinly as possible on a lightly floured surface and, using a cookie cutter or a highball glass, cut circles 3 inches in diameter. Place 1 teaspoon of the meat mixture in the center of each circle. Wet the edges of the dough with a little water, fold in half, and pinch the edges together to seal. Place on greased and floured cookie sheets, and brush with the egg wash.

6. Bake until golden brown, about 30 minutes. Serve hot.

Brisket and Cabbage Soup

Makes 6 to 8 servings

My friend John Scanlon gave me the recipe for this soup more than 35 years ago when we summered on Long Island. We rented a little shack near the beach and had a wonderful time eating, sharing stories, telling jokes, and laughing a lot. His kids and mine were the exact same ages, and they loved the beach. He recently passed away but still holds the title for "raconteur par excellence," and we miss him. This soup is one of many things which carry on his good name. Serve with hot crusty bread, a good salad, and a bottle of red wine. For a stick-to-your-ribs meal on a cold evening, this is it.

Seasoned flour:

1 cup Wondra flour

2 teaspoons garlic salt

1 teaspoon paprika

1 teaspoon dried basil

½ teaspoon freshly ground
  black pepper

3 pounds beef shinbones,
  marrowbones, or soup bones

One 3-pound piece straight-cut beef
  brisket, cut into 3 pieces

2 medium-size onions, chopped

4 large cloves garlic, crushed

1 medium-size head white cabbage,
  cored and thinly sliced

2 medium-size yellow or red beets,
  greens discarded, peeled, and cubed

One 32-ounce can whole tomatoes,
  broken up, with their juices

2 cups beef broth

Juice of 2 lemons

2 tablespoons sugar

10 to 12 small Yukon Gold
  potatoes

Bouquet garni:

6 sprigs fresh parsley

1 bay leaf

½ teaspoon dried basil

1 teaspoon black peppercorns

1 cup sour cream (optional),
  for serving

(continued on page 108)

ELLEN'S TIPS

★ I recommend that you make this soup the day before you plan to serve it. The flavor just gets better.

★ Use the meatiest soup bones for better flavor. Ask your butcher for advice.

★ You can use oregano, sage, or dill in place of basil in the seasoned flour.

(continued from page 107)

★ You should remove the hard blossom ends of the tomatoes when you break them up.

★ Peasant bread—white, brown, or black—tastes wonderful with this soup.

1. Preheat the oven to 400°F.

2. To make the seasoned flour, combine all the ingredients in a shallow bowl.

3. Dredge the shinbones and brisket in the seasoned flour and place in a roasting pan. Bake until browned, turning once, 30 to 40 minutes total. Transfer the browned meat and bones to a large soup pot and add water to cover. Cover and bring to a boil over medium heat.

4. Using the same pan you used to brown the meat and bones, cook the onions and garlic over medium heat, stirring often, until softened, 5 to 7 minutes. Add to the soup pot, along with the cabbage, beets, tomatoes, beef broth, lemon juice, sugar, and potatoes.

5. To make the bouquet garni, tie up all the ingredients in a piece of cheesecloth. Add to the pot. Reduce the heat to low, cover, and simmer, stirring occasionally, until the meat is tender, at least 1½ hours.

6. Discard the bones and bouquet garni. Take out the meat and trim away the fat. Shred the meat into bite-size pieces and return to the pot.

7. Serve in warm bowls with a dollop of sour cream, if desired.

Ellen's Favorite Dressings

Makes about 1 cup

ELLEN'S TIPS

★ Do not refrigerate. Both of these dressings will keep in the cupboard for weeks, but they are so good that they will disappear quickly.

I've been using these two dressings for many years. I can't remember who gave the first version to me, but it is the more versatile. I keep it in a mayonnaise jar, and I never refrigerate it, because the flavor is better if you don't. Trust me. The second version is made with balsamic vinegar, and I love it just as much.

Version 1:

¾ cup olive oil

¼ cup good-quality red wine vinegar

1 teaspoon dry mustard

1 teaspoon salt

1 teaspoon sugar

4 cloves garlic, crushed

Version 2:

¾ cup olive oil

2 tablespoons balsamic vinegar

1 tablespoon good-quality red wine vinegar

1 teaspoon sugar

Put all the ingredients in a jar with a tight-fitting lid and shake well.

Warm Apple Crisp

Makes 8 servings

Every time one of my children came home from college for a vacation, they wanted roast chicken and apple crisp. It was completely predictable. I was happy to comply because the entire meal is no trouble and we love it as well. To them, this is Mama's comfort food. No question—this needs to be topped with Homemade Vanilla Ice Cream (page 113).

2 tablespoons butter, softened

8 Pippin apples

1 tablespoon fresh lemon juice

2 teaspoons grated lemon rind

1 cup firmly packed dark
    brown sugar

1 cup all-purpose flour

¼ teaspoon salt

1 teaspoon ground cinnamon

Topping:

½ cup (1 stick) plus 2 tablespoons
    butter

1. Preheat the oven to 375°F. Use the butter to grease a 9- or 10-inch baking dish.
2. Core, peel, and slice the apples ½ inch thick. Place in the prepared dish and sprinkle with the lemon juice and rind (grate the rind first, then juice the lemon).
3. To make the topping, in a food processor, pulsing on and off, combine ½ cup of the butter, the brown sugar, flour, salt, and cinnamon until the mixture resembles coarse meal. Or do this in a medium-size mixing bowl, mixing everything together with a fork or pastry blender. Sprinkle evenly over the apples. Dot with the remaining 2 tablespoons butter.
4. Bake on the center oven rack until the top is browned and bubbly, about 30 minutes. Serve warm.

Other Types of Apples
   Rome or Granny Smith apples can be used instead of Pippin. It must be a hard apple that will keep its shape.

ELLEN'S TIPS

★ The topping is best when sprinkled on the apples *without* patting or pushing it down. Leave lumps and spaces in between the crumbled topping for the apples to bubble up while baking.

★ To save time, cut your apples in the morning, toss them with the lemon juice and rind, cover, and refrigerate. The crumb topping also can be made ahead, covered, and refrigerated. Assemble the dish for baking right before your guests arrive.

Homemade Vanilla Ice Cream

Makes 1 quart

If you have an ice-cream maker, you will find that this recipe is a real hit with guests. I was always intimidated by the idea of homemade ice cream, but I experimented with quite a few recipes and decided that this one is the best.

2 cups whole milk
¾ cup heavy cream
1 vanilla bean, split lengthwise, or
  1 tablespoon pure vanilla extract

3 large egg yolks
½ cup plus 1 tablespoon sugar

1. In a medium-size saucepan over medium heat, bring the milk, heavy cream, and vanilla bean, if using, to a boil. Remove from the heat. Remove the vanilla bean, scrape the brown seeds out of the inside of the hull, and stir them back into the mixture. Discard the hull.
2. In a large mixing bowl with an electric mixer on medium speed, beat the egg yolks and sugar until the mixture is light yellow. Add about ½ cup of the hot milk mixture to the yolk mixture and stir well. Stir in another ½ cup of the hot mixture, then add the yolk mixture to the saucepan and mix well. Bring to a simmer over low heat; do not let it come to a boil.
3. Remove from the heat. Stir in the vanilla extract, if using, and let cool.
4. Transfer to the ice-cream maker and freeze as directed by the manufacturer.

Variations:
  Add your favorite crunchies after you've made the ice cream but before putting it in the freezer.
  - *½ cup broken-up Heath, Butterfinger, or other praline candy bars*
  - *½ cup semisweet chocolate bits*
  - *½ cup drained and chopped canned chestnuts*
  - *½ cup raisins, soaked in ¼ cup rum until plumped*
  - *½ cup peeled and diced banana and ⅓ cup chopped almonds*
  - *½ cup butterscotch bits or candy*

In freezing April, when we still get snow from time to time, my husband, Joe, starts planting and germinating his seeds in our apartment. He uses our den as his greenhouse, filling it with 10 or 15 flats of sunflowers, radishes, beets, kale, string beans, gourds, cucumbers, and, this year, corn. This last crop was added so that his only grandson could pick his own ears at the end of the summer (despite the fact that you can easily walk down the lane and buy some). Now I know warm weather is coming, the garden will get planted, and our apartment will get back in order. When the plants really get going, Joe harvests and I cook—everything.

At this time of year, you don't have to work really hard to come up with a great meal. You just see what looks the ripest, the brightest, and the freshest. I try to invent new ways of serving and combining foods so that we will have some variety.

I do the same thing with my table. I usually buy something brand-new for the warm weather—new place mats, new napkins, maybe a new set of salad plates—something to pick me up for the coming entertaining season.

I get a lot of inspiration from fresh flowers, and from fresh fruits and vegetables that I haven't seen all year. But it doesn't dissuade me from my consistent belief that simple food is the way to go. I don't need to try the latest sauce or the trendy new cheese that I see everywhere. To my mind, "gourmet" food has become a bit pricey and overly precious.

When the weather gets warm and nice, people like to move around more. Buffet meals, drinks on the terrace, even dessert and coffee outside all make for a casual outdoor meal. Take a look around your own house and see where it might be fun to eat: a screened-in porch, a library, even the backyard. The setting doesn't have to be glamorous or elegantly appointed; it simply has to be comfortable. It's always great to have a pitcher of something to offer, lemonade in pretty glasses or even a cold soup in wine goblets, and perhaps warm cheese squares or some other tasty munchie.

Your table doesn't need a lot of dressing up when you have big bunches of dahlias or zinnias in small pitchers on the table. I use napkins whose colors echo those of the flowers and a few low candles. It doesn't take much of an investment to transform your table.

One year I hosted a square dance as a surprise birthday party for Joe, an Oklahoman by birth. I went to an army-navy store and bought a bunch of different-colored bandannas to use as napkins. I also bought chile pepper lights to string over the table and a nest of harvest baskets with red chile peppers painted on the sides. I used these baskets on the sideboard to hold a bunch of lovely wheat, silverware wrapped in napkins, and corn chips and dip.

When you are doing themes like this, remember that less is more. Just have a good time. Do enough to make a little splash but not so much that it overwhelms you or your guests. Use common sense in every season.

Butterflied Leg of Lamb on the Grill with Fresh Mint Sauce

Makes 8 to 10 servings

This recipe is going to be as good as your butcher and your griller are. The marinating process is important. Although there are as many marinades as there are flowers, I like this one because it is easy and I usually have all the ingredients on hand.

1 whole leg of lamb, boned and
   butterflied (ask your butcher
   to do this)
Salt and freshly ground black pepper
   to taste
3 to 4 large cloves garlic, to your
   taste, sliced

1 tablespoon chopped fresh rosemary
   leaves
2 cups Ellen's Favorite Dressing:
   Version 1 (page 110)
1 large onion, sliced medium thick
Fresh Mint Sauce (page 125)

1. Season both sides of the lamb with salt and pepper. Make eight to ten 1-inch-deep x 2-inch-long slits in the meat and slip a slice of garlic into each. Rub the meat with the rosemary and place in a glass baking dish. Pour on the dressing, making sure to coat all of the lamb, and add the onion. Cover with plastic wrap and let marinate in the refrigerator for a few hours, turning a couple of times.

2. Grill the lamb over a hot fire for about 10 minutes on each side, making sure that the meat doesn't get too well done. Every grill is different, so I use the finger test. When the meat can be pushed in with some resistance, it is medium. If it is hard, it is well done. If it is soft and mushy, it is raw. That's not very scientific, but it usually works.

3. Remove the lamb from the fire and let rest for 5 to 10 minutes to let the juices settle. Slice about ½ inch thick and serve with the mint sauce on the side.

Fresh Mint Sauce

Makes 1 cup

I grow mint every summer in an old wine keg along with other herbs. I always make this sauce when I grill lamb. The mint steeps in a vinegar and sugar syrup until the flavor permeates the mixture. Some people like to leave the mint in the sauce, or you can strain it out. Sometimes I like to swirl the sauce in a blender to get a somewhat smoother consistency.

1 cup white vinegar

3 tablespoons sugar

**6 tablespoons finely chopped
fresh mint leaves**

In a medium-size nonreactive saucepan, bring the vinegar to a boil. Add the sugar, stirring until it dissolves. Stir in the mint leaves, remove from the heat, and let sit for 30 minutes to let the flavors develop. Serve at room temperature or chilled.

Mary's Blond Brownies

Makes 24 brownies

This incredibly sinful brownie recipe comes from my dear old friend, Mary McLaughlin. I used to love going to her apartment for lunch. We saw each other a lot when our children were small. I have used this recipe for more than 35 years, and guests always love it.

1 cup (2 sticks) unsalted butter,
  softened
1 cup firmly packed dark
  brown sugar
1 cup granulated sugar
2 large eggs, at room temperature

1 cup all-purpose flour
1 tablespoon baking powder
Pinch of salt
½ cup chopped pecans
½ cup semisweet chocolate bits
½ cup confectioners' sugar

1. Preheat the oven to 375°F. Grease a 9 x 13-inch baking pan and set aside.
2. In a large mixing bowl with an electric mixer on medium speed, cream together the butter, brown sugar, and granulated sugar until light and fluffy. Add the eggs alternately with the flour, baking powder, and salt, mixing well after each addition. Fold in the pecans and chocolate bits.
3. Pour the batter into the prepared pan and bake for 15 minutes. Reduce the oven temperature to 350°F and bake until golden brown, about 30 minutes more (see Ellen's Tips).
4. Remove from the oven and let cool completely. Sift the confectioners' sugar evenly over the top, then cut into squares.

ELLEN'S TIPS

★ It's hard to tell when these brownies are done. They will be kind of loose in the center when you pull them out of the oven, but they will set up later as they cool. They are best eaten the next day.

Bridge Snack for the Girls
Before or After the Winnings

Tamale Pie

Baked Fudge and crisp apples

Tamale Pie is a perfect taste treat, and I make it for dinner often. My family loves it because it's crispy and flavorful, sort of like a taco casserole. It's also very filling, with seasoned chopped meat, cheese, and spicy sauce. For our bridge game, it's ideal because it can be served on one plate and isn't difficult to eat. I cut the fudge into very small squares for the card table and serve it with slices of Red Delicious apples, which are very white inside and very sweet. I think the combination of cold, crisp apples and fudge candy helps you to think more efficiently and make your bridge contracts with ease.

Tamale Pie

Makes 6 to 8 servings

This recipe has nothing to do with traditional tamales, but it is one of the tastiest, quickest school-night dinners I have ever made. Everyone loves it, old or young, and it deserves a try.

1 teaspoon canola oil

2 pounds ground beef

One 16-ounce package broad egg noodles

1 tablespoon butter

Sauce:

2 cups canned crushed tomatoes

Two 4.5-ounce cans green chiles, drained and chopped

One 6-ounce can black olives, drained, pitted, and chopped (1½ cups)

½ cup chopped onion

4 cups coarsely crushed tortilla chips (6 ounces)

¾ cup shredded cheddar cheese

⅓ cup freshly grated Parmesan cheese

1. Preheat the oven to 350°F.
2. In a large skillet over medium-high heat, heat the oil. Add the ground beef and cook, breaking up any clumps, until no longer pink, 3 to 4 minutes. Drain off the fat and set aside.
3. In a large pot of lightly salted water, cook the noodles until tender. Drain and toss with the butter.
4. To make the sauce, combine all the ingredients in a medium-size saucepan over medium heat. Bring to a simmer, reducing the heat to low if necessary, and continue to cook.
5. In a lightly oiled 10- to 12-inch square baking dish that is 2 to 3 inches deep, layer half the noodles, tortilla chips, meat, sauce, and cheddar cheese. Repeat with the remaining noodles, chips, meat, sauce, and cheddar, then sprinkle with the Parmesan.
6. Bake until the cheese is melted and bubbling, about 30 minutes. Serve immediately.

Splendid Curry Extravaganza
Engagement Dinner for 12

Pimm's Cup

Parsleyed Green Beans

Spicy Grilled Shrimp

Chicken Curry with Condiments

Poori

Coconut Cake with an Orchid

To celebrate the engagement of my son, David, and his gorgeous fiancée, Celine, I decided to show off a bit. I dressed up my table with a favorite embroidered cloth and pewter chargers that I had bought in Mexico. Pimm's Cup was a must for this dinner. I have a collection of pewter and glass mugs that I use for this drink and I always add a cucumber spear to the glass to double as a crunchy swizzle stick. I put my old wooden twisted candlesticks with brass shades on the table, and at each place setting was my version of place cards: a *New Yorker* cartoon that targets each person's peculiarities. Nowadays, the only drawback is that I have to put reading glasses at the table for people to get the jokes.

Serving an Indian meal is always a treat because most people don't cook this kind of food at home. Several of these recipes were inspired by Madhur Jaffrey, my Indian cooking teacher. I used to ask her where we could go to get a good Indian meal, and her answer was always the same: home.

Pimm's Cup

Makes 8 drinks

I first had this drink in San Francisco in 1958 at a restaurant called The India House. It was served with a long, unpeeled cucumber spear in a pewter mug and was perfect with the curry. It is a great summer drink that goes well with anything, but curry cries for it.

Ice

8 ounces Pimm's Cup
(see Ellen's Tips)

1 quart ginger ale

1 medium-size cucumber, unpeeled and cut into 8 spears, for garnish

8 sprigs fresh mint (optional), for garnish

Place a handful of ice in each of eight 8-ounce glasses. Add 1 ounce of the Pimm's Cup and fill with ginger ale. Garnish with a cucumber spear and a mint sprig, if using.

Parsleyed Green Beans

Makes 6 to 8 servings

This is a simple but satisfying way to make green beans. I prefer to use curly parsley in this recipe, as it gives the beans a very fresh taste.

1 pound green beans, ends trimmed

2 tablespoons butter

3 tablespoons chopped fresh curly parsley leaves

Bring a large saucepan of salted water to a boil. Add the string beans and cook until barely tender to the point of a sharp knife. Drain and transfer to a warm serving bowl. Add the butter and toss well to distribute. Add the parsley and toss again. Serve immediately.

Spicy Grilled Shrimp

Makes 6 to 8 servings

This is my version of a recipe I saw on television when I lived in Florida. Jacques Pépin was doing the demonstration in his cute French accent. It is, beyond a doubt, the best shrimp I have ever had. The shrimp are marinated in spicy herbs, then pan-grilled quickly in a dry skillet and sometimes served with spinach as a first course. The herbs make a nice balance to the curry dish to follow.

3½ pounds jumbo shrimp, peeled and deveined, if necessary (see Ellen's Tips)
2 tablespoons olive oil
½ teaspoon dried thyme
½ teaspoon dried oregano
¼ teaspoon ground coriander
¼ teaspoon red pepper flakes
1 teaspoon fresh lemon juice
2 cloves garlic, chopped
Salt and freshly ground black pepper to taste

1. Place the shrimp in a glass pie plate. Drizzle with the oil and sprinkle with the thyme, oregano, coriander, red pepper flakes, lemon juice, garlic, and salt and pepper. Turn the shrimp in the mixture to coat evenly. Cover with plastic wrap and let marinate in the refrigerator overnight.
2. Heat a large cast-iron skillet over high heat until good and hot. Place the shrimp in the skillet, shaking off excess marinade. Cook, turning once, until pink, about 2 minutes per side. Remove from the heat.
3. Serve hot or at room temperature, on a plate with a small container of toothpicks and a lemon half to hold the "used" toothpicks.

ELLEN'S TIPS

★ I devein shrimp only when the veins are obvious. Use a sharp knife to gently slit the back, and rinse under cold running water.

★ Do not overcook the shrimp. They will get rubbery and tough if you do.

Chicken Curry with Condiments

Makes 12 servings

Over the years, I've changed, tested, and combined four different curry recipes to create this one, which I think is a winner. Don't be scared off by the number of ingredients. It comes together easily, and the end result is worth the extra time.

5 pounds chicken breasts and thighs,
   cut into serving-size pieces
Salt and freshly ground black
   pepper to taste
11 tablespoons butter
3 tablespoons vegetable oil
2 medium-size onions, cut into several
   pieces
4 large cloves garlic, peeled
2 medium-size carrots, finely diced
¼ cup freshly purchased mild
   curry powder

½ teaspoon ground cinnamon
¼ teaspoon ground cloves
One 1-inch piece fresh ginger, peeled
Pinch of saffron threads
3 cups chicken broth
One 14-ounce can unsweetened
   coconut milk
1 cup canned crushed tomatoes
1 cup heavy cream
6 cups cooked long-grain white rice
   (preferably basmati)
Condiments of your choice (page 138)

1. Season the chicken pieces with salt and pepper.
2. In a large frying pan over medium heat, heat 3 tablespoons of the butter and the vegetable oil together until the butter melts. Add the seasoned chicken pieces in batches and brown on both sides.
3. Place the onions, garlic, carrots, curry powder, cinnamon, cloves, ginger, and saffron in a food processor and process into a coarse paste.
4. In a medium-size skillet over medium heat, heat the remaining 8 tablespoons butter until it melts and bubbles. Reduce the heat to medium-low, add the spice paste, and cook until lightly browned, 2 to 3 minutes. Whisk in the chicken broth, coconut

★ You can make your own curry powder by mixing together equal amounts of ground cumin, ground coriander, and ground turmeric, all freshly purchased. It is, in fact, quite a bit better than purchased curry powder.

★ Most spices lose their flavor after about 4 months on the shelf.

★ This is definitely better made the day before and reheated.

milk, tomatoes, and heavy cream and cook until thickened. Add the chicken pieces, cover, reduce the heat to low, and cook until the chicken is falling off the bone, about 1 hour.

5. Serve on a platter with the rice piled in the center, the chicken around the edge, and some sauce drizzled over the chicken only. Serve extra sauce in a gravy boat. Include your choice of condiments in separate bowls.

Basmati Rice

This rice is no longer hard to get. I found it recently at my large supermarket. Just follow the package directions; there are no tricks. Figure 1 cup uncooked rice to 2 cups water for 4 people.

The Condiments

This is always the best part of a curry meal because you can make it as dressy or as plain as you want. Be sure to put these condiments in pretty little bowls on a tray, with a different small spoon for each. My favorite spoons are carved wooden ones I have collected over the years in my travels. Your grandmother's or mother's old mismatched ones also would look great.

- *2 cups raisins (preferably golden), soaked in hot water to cover for 1 hour and drained*
- *2 cups unsalted dry-roasted peanuts, chopped*
- *2 cups mango chutney*
- *1 cup sweetened shredded coconut, toasted on an ungreased baking sheet in a 350°F oven until light golden brown, about 20 minutes*
- *1 cup peeled and chopped banana (optional)*
- *1 cup Tomato Onion Relish (recipe follows)*
- *2 cups Cucumber and Yogurt Raita (page 141)*

Tomato Onion Relish

Makes 2 cups

This relish has evolved over 10 years of fooling around with the ingredients and amounts. It also pairs wonderfully with chops or burgers.

1 medium-size ripe tomato, cut into
    ¼-inch dice
1 medium-size onion, finely chopped
½ teaspoon salt
¼ teaspoon freshly ground
    white pepper

1 generous tablespoon fresh
    lemon juice
1 teaspoon seeded and finely diced
    hot green chile
Pinch of cayenne pepper

Combine all the ingredients in a medium-size serving bowl. Cover with plastic wrap and refrigerate for at least 30 minutes for the flavors to develop. Serve within a few hours of making, at room temperature.

ELLEN'S TIPS

★ This relish does not keep. The tomatoes get soggy, and the onions don't stay crisp. It must be served the same day it is made.

Cucumber and Yogurt Raita

Makes about 4 cups

This sauce is essential as a cooling counterpoint to the hot, spicy curry. It can be used as a dip for other occasions.

1 large cucumber

½ teaspoon cumin seeds

One 16-ounce container plain yogurt

1 teaspoon salt

⅛ teaspoon freshly ground black pepper

⅛ teaspoon cayenne pepper

⅛ teaspoon paprika, for garnish

1. Peel the cucumber and cut in half lengthwise. Scrape out the seeds and grate medium-coarse. Place in a strainer, weight with a heavy teakettle filled with water or a similar object, and let the water drain out for at least 1 hour.
2. In a small skillet over medium heat, heat the cumin seeds until they pop. Grind them in a small grinder and set the powder aside.
3. In a medium-size serving bowl, beat the yogurt until smooth. Add the cucumber, salt, black pepper, cumin, and cayenne and mix together well. Cover with plastic wrap and refrigerate until ready to serve. Sprinkle with the paprika just before serving.

ELLEN'S TIPS

★ This needs to be eaten the day it is made. The cucumber makes it watery if it's kept any longer.

★ You may substitute ground cumin for the freshly heated and ground seeds.

Poori

Makes 12 breads

Poori is made from scratch, but that's not difficult to do, and the return on your investment is huge. You will love the result, and everyone will admire your skill. Only you and I will know how easy it is.

1 cup all-purpose flour

1 cup whole wheat flour

2 tablespoons vegetable oil, plus
   more for frying

1 teaspoon salt

½ cup warm water (about 110°F;
   see Ellen's Tips)

1. Combine all the ingredients in a food processor, pulsing until the mixture forms a ball, only a few seconds. Turn out onto a lightly floured work surface and knead for about 10 minutes. Oil the dough and place it in a plastic bag for 30 minutes.
2. Divide the dough into 12 equal-size balls. On a lightly floured work surface, roll each one out to about 5 inches in diameter.
3. In a small, deep frying pan over medium-high heat, heat 1 inch of vegetable oil until hot but not smoking. Reduce the heat a little and fry one dough round at a time. It will puff up like a balloon and brown quickly. Flip it over to cook for a second on the other side, then transfer to a plate lined with paper towels to drain. Serve immediately.

Indian Breads

Bread is an essential component of any Indian meal. In addition to poori, which is made from scratch, you might try poppadums or pappadams, thin East Indian breads made with lentil flour. Poppadums are sold in stacks, like tortillas, and can be found in Indian groceries. Right before serving, grill them in a hot, dry skillet for 10 to 20 seconds per side.

ELLEN'S TIPS

★ To make sure the oil is ready, drop a tiny amount of water in the oil. If it "spits," it's ready.

★ The dough for the poori can be made a day ahead and kept refrigerated until you cook them.

★ The poori must be made and served within 30 minutes. The breads won't stay puffed up for very long.

★ If you don't have a thermometer for the water, use my "finger test." Dip your pinkie into the water; if you don't feel anything—not cold, cool, or hot— it is just the right temperature.

Coconut Cake with an Orchid

Makes one 10-inch tube cake;

16 regular servings or 12 huge servings

I was introduced to this gorgeous cake by Alison Mesrop, a wonderful chef, who made it for dessert one evening. The people at the table couldn't believe how beautiful it was and how good it tasted. Remember, the orchid is meant for ornamentation only, not for nibbling!

Filling:

3 cups unsweetened coconut milk

6 large egg yolks, at room temperature (reserve the whites for the icing)

1 cup sugar

¼ cup cornstarch

2 teaspoons pure coconut extract

Cake:

2 cups (4 sticks) unsalted butter, softened

2⅓ cups sugar

1 teaspoon pure vanilla extract

2 teaspoons pure coconut extract

8 large eggs, at room temperature

½ cup unsweetened coconut milk

1½ cups unsweetened shredded coconut (available at health food stores)

3 cups cake flour

2 teaspoons baking powder

½ teaspoon salt

Icing:

4 cups sugar

2 cups water

6 large egg whites, at room temperature

1 cup unsweetened shredded coconut, toasted on an ungreased baking sheet in a 350°F oven until light golden brown, about 20 minutes

1 orchid or other flat flower, for garnish

ELLEN'S TIPS

★ To make this job easier, prepare the filling and icing ahead of time. The cake can be made the day before and wrapped in plastic when completely cool.

★ To cut the cake into 3 thin layers, use a long serrated knife and cut in a sawing motion. If the cake is cool, it won't crumble and break.

★ Toast the coconut for the topping in advance, let cool completely, and store in an airtight container until needed.

(continued on page 145)

1. To make the filling, heat the coconut milk in a large, heavy saucepan over medium heat until bubbles begin to form at the edge of the pan; do not let it come to a boil.

In a large mixing bowl, whisk together the egg yolks, sugar, and cornstarch until light and smooth. Slowly add the hot milk, whisking constantly. Return the mixture to the saucepan and bring to a boil over medium heat. Cook until thickened, about 10 seconds. Strain through a fine-mesh strainer and stir in the coconut extract. Let cool, then refrigerate for at least 6 hours or overnight.

2. Preheat the oven to 350°F. Butter and flour a 10-inch tube pan, knocking out the excess flour.

3. To make the cake, place the butter and sugar in a large mixing bowl. Using an electric mixer on medium speed, beat until fluffy. Add the extracts, then add the eggs one at a time, beating well after each addition. Add the coconut milk and shredded coconut and beat until smooth, scraping down the sides of the bowl.

4. In a medium-size mixing bowl, sift together the cake flour, baking powder, and salt and add to the butter-sugar mixture. Beat on medium speed until smooth. Transfer the batter to the prepared pan and bake on the center oven rack until a cake tester comes out clean, about 1 hour. Remove from the oven and let cool on a wire rack for 10 minutes before turning the cake out of the pan.

5. To make the icing, in a large saucepan over medium to high heat, bring the sugar and water to a boil. Continue to boil, stirring, until the sugar dissolves, about 5 minutes. In a large stainless steel mixing bowl with an electric mixer on high speed, beat the egg whites until glossy peaks form when you lift the beaters, about 5 minutes. Add the hot sugar syrup slowly in a thin stream while beating on high speed. Continue to beat until the mixture is cool to the touch, about 20 minutes. The icing may be made up to 4 hours ahead of assembly.

6. To assemble the cake, cut the cooled cake horizontally into 3 layers. Place 1 layer on a pretty cake plate and spread half the filling on top. Repeat with another layer and the remaining filling. Top with the third layer and spread some of the icing thickly on the sides. Mound the remaining icing on top, using a spoon to make dents and peaks. Take a handful of toasted coconut and gently tilt the palm of your hand toward the sides of the cake to make the coconut stick. Sprinkle the top with the remaining coconut. Garnish with the orchid.

ELLEN'S TIPS

(continued from page 143)

★ Don't add the hot milk too quickly to the egg yolk mixture, or it will scramble. If it does, add 1 tablespoon boiling water and beat quickly until it comes together.

★ The filling may be made 1 to 2 days ahead. The assembly can be done up to 3 hours before serving.

Tomato and Basil Bruschetta

Makes 6 to 8 servings

I love these little toasts. I could actually make a meal out of bruschetta. I think rubbing the toast with garlic really adds to the flavor.

1 loaf French bread
4 cloves garlic, peeled
½ cup extra virgin olive oil,
   or as needed

2 medium-size ripe tomatoes
1 tablespoon chopped fresh
   basil leaves

1. Preheat the oven to 200°F.
2. Cut the bread diagonally into 1-inch-thick slices. Place the slices on ungreased cookie sheets and bake, turning once after 10 minutes, until they are hard and golden, about 20 minutes total. Rub each slice with garlic and brush lightly with olive oil. Set aside.
3. Dice the tomatoes. In a small mixing bowl, combine the tomatoes, 2 tablespoons of the olive oil, and the basil. Spoon 1 tablespoon of the mixture onto each slice of bread, patting the tomatoes down so they will stay in place. Serve at once.

Soni's Chicken Provençal

Makes 6 to 8 servings

ELLEN'S TIPS

★ Don't be alarmed. The vegetables may look overcooked, but they taste great.

★ The artichoke hearts can go into the pan slightly thawed, just enough so that you can break them apart.

★ Warn your guests that the olives have pits in them.

Soni is one of my dearest friends. We had our first children at exactly the same time in San Francisco. Her children were surprise twins, and mine was just the usual shocking one. She entertains a great deal and goes to great lengths to please her company. I have used this wonderful recipe of hers for years. It is a quick dish to assemble and is great with hot, crusty French bread to dunk in the gravy.

10 to 12 large shallots, chopped

One 32-ounce can whole tomatoes, with their juices

1 head garlic, broken apart but not peeled

⅔ cup black Niçoise or Greek olives, drained

Two 9-ounce packages frozen artichoke hearts (see Ellen's Tips)

⅓ cup fresh lemon juice

½ cup olive oil

1 tablespoon chopped fresh rosemary leaves or 1 teaspoon dried

1 tablespoon chopped fresh thyme leaves or 1 teaspoon dried

Salt and freshly ground black pepper to taste

1 to 2 cups chicken broth, as needed

Two 4-pound chickens, cut into serving-size pieces

1. Preheat the oven to 350°F.
2. Place the shallots, tomatoes, garlic, olives, and artichoke hearts in a roasting pan. Pour the lemon juice and olive oil over them, sprinkle with the rosemary and thyme, season with salt and pepper, and add 1 cup of the chicken broth. Cover the pan with aluminum foil and bake for 20 minutes.
3. Season the chicken with salt and pepper and add to the pan. Cover and roast for 45 minutes, basting often with the pan juices and adding more chicken broth, if necessary, to keep the bird moist.
4. Increase the oven temperature to 400°F, uncover the pan, and roast until the chicken is golden brown, about 15 minutes more.
5. Arrange the chicken on a warm platter and spoon the softened vegetables around it. Ladle on some of the pan sauce and serve.

Smashed Red Potatoes

Makes 6 to 8 servings

I love red potatoes cooked in almost any manner, but this way is spectacular. My daughter Lexie, an architect and mother of two little girls, makes this often. Even her picky eaters love it. I hope you like it as much as they do.

12 large red potatoes
Salt to taste
½ cup (1 stick) butter
⅔ cup sour cream

⅔ cup freshly grated Parmesan cheese
½ cup heavy cream, warmed
Freshly ground black pepper
  to taste

1. Wash the potatoes well and place them in a large pot with plenty of cold water. Add a pinch of salt, bring to a boil, and continue to boil until they are fork tender, about 30 minutes.
2. Drain and coarsely mash the potatoes in the pot with a hand masher. Add the butter, sour cream, Parmesan, and heavy cream and mash for another minute or so, until everything is well mixed. Season with salt and pepper. Cover and keep warm in a low oven until ready to serve.

Warm Spinach Salad

Makes 6 to 8 servings

I love the warm dressing on the cold spinach leaves: it is always a surprise. If you add hard-boiled eggs to this salad, it makes a wonderful main-course salad for a special lunch.

2 pounds fresh spinach

4 to 5 strips bacon

½ cup Ellen's Favorite Dressing:
   Version 1 (page 110)

2 hard-boiled eggs (optional),
   quartered

1. Wash the spinach well, soaking the leaves in the sink with plenty of cold water to remove all the sand. Snap off the tough stems. Spin the leaves dry or pat them dry with paper towels. Place in a large salad bowl and cover with a clean kitchen towel. Refrigerate until serving time.
2. Cook the bacon until crisp and place on paper towels to drain. Set aside.
3. Right before serving, warm the dressing in a small saucepan over low heat. Pour it over the spinach and toss. Crumble the bacon at the last minute, add to the salad, and toss again. Garnish with the egg quarters, if using, and serve at once.

The Perfect Hard-Boiled Egg

To hard-boil eggs perfectly, place the eggs in a medium-size saucepan, add cold water to cover, and bring to a boil over high heat. Turn off the heat, cover, and let sit for 15 minutes, then rinse with cold water. This method keeps the yolks yellow, without that green tinge.

ELLEN'S TIPS

★ You can wash the spinach the day before to save time.

★ You can buy pre-washed spinach leaves, but you still need to rinse them at least once.

★ You can cook the bacon and hard-boiled eggs earlier in the day and hold the eggs in the refrigerator until serving time.

★ Toss the salad at the last minute so the leaves won't wilt too much.

Sweet Corn Cakes with Berries and Cream

Makes 6 to 8 servings

I got this delicious recipe from a friend several summers ago. It was served with assorted berries, but I prefer one kind of berry for a cleaner taste. These corn cakes make wonderful breakfast food, toasted and slathered with butter and honey.

1 cup (2 sticks) plus 2 tablespoons
   unsalted butter, softened

1 cup sugar

3 tablespoons dark or light corn syrup

4 large eggs, at room temperature

1½ cups yellow cornmeal

1¾ cups all-purpose flour

½ teaspoon salt

2 teaspoons baking powder

1 cup heavy cream

1 tablespoon water

3 cups fresh blackberries, raspberries,
   or blueberries, or a combination,
   picked over

2 cups heavy cream, whipped to
   soft peaks

1. Preheat the oven to 375°F. Butter an 8-inch square baking pan and dust with flour, knocking out the excess flour. Set aside.

2. In a large mixing bowl with an electric mixer on medium speed, beat the butter and ¾ cup of the sugar until light and fluffy, about 3 minutes. Add the corn syrup, then add the eggs one at a time, beating well after each addition.

3. In a medium-size mixing bowl, combine the cornmeal, flour, salt, and baking powder. Add this alternately with the cream to the butter mixture.

4. Pour the batter into the prepared baking dish. Brush with some of the water and sprinkle evenly with the remaining ¼ cup sugar. Bake until a cake tester inserted in the center comes out clean, 40 to 45 minutes.

5. Let cool, then cut the cake into large squares. To serve, split each square horizontally, top one half with some blackberries, add the other half, and finish with a spoonful of whipped cream.

ELLEN'S TIPS

★ You may substitute honey or maple syrup for the corn syrup.

★ Another way to test the cake is to press the center with your finger. If it springs back, it's done.

★ I don't put any sugar or vanilla extract in my whipped cream, but some people like it that way. It's your choice.

★ Do not wash blackberries or raspberries.

Brunch for Whoever's Around

Before the Mass Exodus

Mimosas and Bloody Marys

Minted Fresh Fruit Salad

Chicken, Potato, and Onion Hash

Puffy Eggs in Casserole

Crisp toasted Rancho Bread

Aunt Stella's Streusel Coffee Cake

Sunday is the day when everyone is getting ready to leave after a weekend visit. Whether it is family or friends, they are happy to indulge in a nice brunch to say goodbye before heading home. A brunch like this one has something for everyone, hungry and not-so-hungry, designated driver and otherwise.

We start with mimosas or the best bloody marys known to man—spicy and with an optional small beer chaser. The hash and eggs are of the stick-to-your-ribs variety, and the toast is unforgettable. A piece of Aunt Stella's coffee cake, washed down with a good cup of coffee, is not to be missed. All in all, a worthy meal.

Mimosas

Makes 10 to 12 drinks

The mimosa is a no-recipe recipe, but one that requires fresh orange juice and halfway decent champagne or sparkling wine. It's the juice and fizz that set your appetite humming.

8 cups fresh orange juice (from 10 to 12 juice oranges)

One 750-ml bottle champagne

In your prettiest champagne flutes, combine a jigger of champagne and ½ cup juice. Serve immediately.

ELLEN'S TIPS

★ Anything looks good in a pretty champagne flute, but fresh orange juice guarantees wonderful flavor as well.

★ These are also very nice using ruby red grapefruit juice instead of orange juice. If you are lucky enough to get blood oranges, use them instead.

★ Be sure to keep the champagne refrigerated until serving. Freeze the champagne glasses ahead of time, too, if you wish.

Bloody Marys

Makes 8 to 10 drinks

Not to sound conceited, but I have become famous for my bloody marys. I make the mix in a pitcher with good-quality tomato juice (I like Sacramento brand) and lots of spices. I decorate the drinks with long, crisp celery sticks—the young, pale green ones with the leaves left on. Mugs are perfect for this drink, although it is also pretty in a wineglass.

The latest additions to my recipe are a rim of finely ground black pepper (like salt on a margarita glass) and a small beer chaser to put out the fire. Use a light beer instead of a darker one for the chaser.

1 large strip lemon peel
½ cup freshly and finely ground
    black pepper
One 46-ounce can tomato juice
2 tablespoons fresh lemon juice
1 tablespoon Worcestershire sauce
2 tablespoons prepared white
    horseradish

Tabasco sauce to taste
1 teaspoon celery salt
½ teaspoon freshly ground
    white pepper
8 to 10 ounces vodka
Ice
8 to 10 thin inner celery ribs,
    with leaves, for garnish

1. Prepare the glasses by wetting the rims with the outside of the lemon peel and turning them in a plate containing the black pepper.
2. Place the tomato juice, lemon juice, Worcestershire, horseradish, Tabasco, celery salt, and white pepper in a large pitcher and mix well. Keep at room temperature.
3. Pour 1 ounce of the vodka over ice into a prepared glass and fill with the tomato juice mixture. Garnish with a celery rib and serve.

Minted Fresh Fruit Salad

Makes 10 to 12 servings

Make this your own way. I like to cut up the fruit the night before to save time on the day of my party. For a buffet, serve the salad in little bowls that fit on the plate, or even a small, wide-mouthed glass. Add the chopped fresh mint for a flavor kick.

1 ripe cantaloupe, honeydew melon, or Crenshaw melon, halved, seeded, peeled, and cut into bite-size chunks

1 pint ripe strawberries, hulled and quartered

1 pint blueberries, picked over for stems

One 8-ounce can sliced peaches, with their juices, cut into bite-size chunks

2 ripe Anjou, Bartlett, or Comice pears, peeled, cored, and cut into bite-size chunks

1 cup orange juice

⅓ cup chopped fresh mint leaves, for garnish

1. Combine all the ingredients except the mint, if using, in a serving dish. Cover with plastic wrap and refrigerate until ready to serve.
2. Before serving, garnish with the mint.

Chicken, Potato, and Onion Hash

Makes 8 servings

I began doing hash this way several years ago when I wanted to use leftover roast chicken in a creative way. I serve it with Best Homemade Mustard (page 52). It makes for a great family meal and is fun to serve to like-minded friends. You can chop everything ahead of time and keep it in plastic bags. Or you can prepare the entire thing the day before and recrisp it right before serving. Ideally, it should be like a crunchy pancake filled with the chicken, onions, and potatoes.

2 tablespoons butter

2 tablespoons canola oil

1 large or 2 medium-size onions, cut into ½-inch pieces

1 large Idaho potato or 3 medium-size russet or Yukon Gold potatoes, peeled and cut into ½-inch cubes

3 cups cubed (½ inch) cooked chicken

Salt and freshly ground black pepper to taste

½ cup leftover chicken gravy or chicken broth

1. In a large skillet over medium-high heat, heat the butter and oil together until the butter bubbles. Add the onion and cook, stirring with a wooden spoon, until transparent, about 4 minutes. Add the potatoes and cook, shaking the pan, until lightly browned, about 3 minutes. Add the chicken and mix. Season with salt and pepper. Add the gravy and mix thoroughly. Press down lightly with a spoon, cover, and cook over low to medium heat until the potatoes are cooked through, about 10 minutes. Shake the pan from time to time to keep the hash from sticking.

2. Uncover the pan, weight the hash with a teakettle filled with water or another heavy object (see Ellen's Tips), and cook for about 10 minutes more. When the pancake is ready, the bottom will be browned. You can slide it onto a plate and then back into the pan for a few more minutes to brown the other side.

3. Serve immediately, cut into wedges like a pie.

ELLEN'S TIPS

★ Put a piece of waxed paper or aluminum foil between the hash and the teakettle or other weight. A brick covered with aluminum foil works well, as does a fat can of tomatoes.

★ If your hash doesn't crisp sufficiently to make a "sliding" pancake, bring the pan right to the table and serve the hash with a spoon. There's no shame in that.

Puffy Eggs in Casserole

Makes 8 to 10 servings

This delightful brunch recipe is from Connie Plepler, my son-in-law Andrew's mother. She is a good cook who has been pleasing her family and friends for many years. This dish is best assembled the night before—that's its great claim to fame. It's a real winner for a simple and satisfying brunch.

1 loaf French bread

2 tablespoons butter, softened

12 large eggs, at room temperature, lightly beaten

1 cup shredded sharp cheddar cheese

½ cup whole milk

¼ cup (½ stick) butter, melted

3 tablespoons chopped fresh parsley leaves, for garnish

6 strips bacon, cooked until crisp, drained on paper towels, and crumbled, for garnish

1. The night before serving, cut the bread into 1-inch-thick slices and spread with the softened butter. Butter a large oval or round baking dish that is 2 to 3 inches deep. Layer the bread in the dish, then add the beaten eggs, cheese, milk, and melted butter. Cover with plastic wrap and refrigerate overnight.

2. In the morning, remove the dish from the refrigerator and let sit at room temperature for about 1 hour. Preheat the oven to 325°F.

3. Bake until golden brown and puffy, 50 to 60 minutes. Garnish with the parsley and bacon and serve immediately.

Rancho Bread

Makes 2 loaves

ELLEN'S TIPS

★ It is important to buy fresh yeast. If the yeast mixture doesn't bubble, it means your yeast has kicked the bucket, and you'll need to start over with new yeast.

★ If the water you use to make the bread is too cold, it won't activate the yeast; if it's too hot, it will kill the yeast. The temperature of the water should be about 110°F. If you don't have a thermometer, use my "finger test." Dip your pinkie into the water; if you don't feel anything—not cold, cool, or hot—it is just the right temperature.

I first tasted this great bread at Rancho La Puerta, a spa in Baja California. The bread is amazingly tasty and crunchy when toasted because of the poppy seeds. Some people are terrified of making bread because of the yeast factor, but this one is almost foolproof.

3 cups warm water (about 110°F; see Ellen's Tips)
¼ cup honey
1 package active dry yeast or ¼ ounce fresh cake yeast (check the expiration date for freshness)
8½ to 9½ cups whole wheat flour, as needed

½ cup canola oil
1 cup bran
2½ tablespoons poppy seeds
1½ teaspoons salt
1 large egg, beaten

1. Pour the water into a medium-size mixing bowl and stir in the honey. Sprinkle on the yeast and stir until dissolved. Let sit until bubbles form on top, about 5 minutes.
2. In a large mixing bowl, combine 8½ cups of the flour, the oil, bran, poppy seeds, salt, and yeast mixture. Mix with a wooden spoon until the dough comes together. Transfer to a lightly floured work surface and knead until elastic, adding more flour if the dough is sticky. (If you have a standing mixer, use a dough hook and mix until the dough becomes elastic and pulls away from the sides of the bowl, about 15 minutes.) Shape the dough into a ball and put it in a lightly oiled bowl. Turn the dough in the oil until it is coated, then cover with a clean dishtowel. Let sit in a warm, dry place until doubled in size, about 1 hour.
3. Preheat the oven to 350°F. Lightly oil two 9 x 5-inch loaf pans.
4. Punch the dough down and knead it on a lightly floured surface for 2 to 3 minutes. Cut the dough in half and put each half in one of the prepared pans. With a sharp knife, make three or four 3-inch-long diagonal cuts in the top of the loaves. Cover

with a clean dishtowel and let sit in a warm, dry place until doubled in size, about 45 minutes. Brush the tops with the beaten egg.

5. Bake on the center oven rack until golden brown and a cake tester or sharp knife inserted in the center comes out clean, 35 to 40 minutes.

6. Let cool in the pans for about 20 minutes, then invert onto wire racks and let cool completely before slicing.

★ There are several other cues that will tell you the bread is done. It will sound hollow when you knock your knuckle on top, and it will pull away from the sides of the pan. Also, I can tell bread is done when I begin to smell it.

★ You can freeze the second loaf after it cools completely. Some people like to slice it before freezing so they can just pop the frozen slices in the toaster.

★ You can prepare this bread a day or two ahead.

Gypsy Goulash

Makes 6 to 8 servings

When I learned to cook in the early 1960s, I used the *Gourmet* cookbooks, volumes 1 and 2, which is where I found this recipe—one that I have changed to my own tastes over these many years. Sirloin cut into thick strips, much like the shape of a finger, is the best type of meat to use. I like to serve this over Perfect Buttered Noodles (page 57) with a crisp-cooked vegetable and melon slices to add a bit of color. I have made this goulash for as many as 70 people. You can do this, too, for a big party. Just add the sour cream at the end.

2 tablespoons all-purpose flour

1½ tablespoons paprika

2 teaspoons salt

3 pounds beef sirloin, trimmed of
    fat and cut into 3-inch-long x
    ½-inch-wide strips

3 tablespoons vegetable shortening

6 medium-size onions, thinly sliced

2 cups red wine

2½ cups sour cream

1. Preheat the oven to 350°F.
2. Mix the flour, paprika, and salt together in a small dish. Dust the beef strips evenly with the mixture. In a large, heavy skillet over medium-high heat, heat the shortening until melted. Brown the meat in the hot fat a few pieces at a time. Using a slotted spoon or tongs, transfer to a casserole.
3. Once all the meat is browned, in the same skillet over medium heat, brown the onions, deglazing the pan and scraping up the browned bits as they cook. Transfer to the casserole. Add ½ cup of the wine to the skillet and continue to deglaze the pan. Pour into the casserole along with the remaining 1½ cups wine and 1¼ cups of the sour cream. Stir to combine.
4. Cover and bake until the meat is tender, 1 to 2 hours. (It can be prepared up to this point and refrigerated or frozen for a day or more. When ready to serve, reheat in a 300°F oven for 1 hour.) Stir in the remaining 1¼ cups sour cream 30 minutes before serving. Serve hot.

ELLEN'S TIPS

★ If the sour cream curdles while you are heating it—that is, if it separates, or "breaks," as the French say—add a few tablespoons of boiling water and whisk until the gravy comes back together. The trick is not to heat the sour cream too much.

Plum Tart

Makes 6 to 8 servings

ELLEN'S TIPS

★ I sometimes make this tart by cutting a fluted opening in the top crust, so you can see the plums. It is just as good that way and even a little prettier.

★ If you want to make a more formal presentation, use a tart pan.

★ You also can make little individual tarts by rolling out smaller circles of dough, which is a nice option when serving 2 to 3 people.

During the summer and early fall, when small Italian prune plums are in season, I love to make this tart. The plums have a wonderful taste, and they are a beautiful color—purple skin, gold flesh. You can serve it with mascarpone, crème fraîche, or plain old vanilla ice cream. This tart is rustic country style in feeling, not like the usual classic French one.

12 firm, ripe prune plums or dark plums (2 pounds), halved and pitted
⅓ cup sugar
1 teaspoon ground cinnamon
½ teaspoon freshly grated nutmeg

2 tablespoons unsalted butter, cut into small pieces
1 recipe Foolproof Piecrust (page 83), refrigerated for at least 30 minutes

1. Preheat the oven to 350°F. Butter a large baking dish and cookie sheet and set aside.
2. In a large mixing bowl, sprinkle the plums with 3 tablespoons of the sugar, the cinnamon, and nutmeg and toss to coat evenly. Transfer to the prepared baking dish and dot with the butter. Bake for 15 minutes. Using a slotted spoon, transfer the plums to a large bowl. Pour the juice in the baking dish into a small saucepan and reduce by one-half over medium-low heat, about 5 minutes.
3. Divide the piecrust into 2 even-size balls. Roll out 1 ball on a lightly floured work surface to about ¼ inch thick. Transfer to the prepared cookie sheet and place the cooked plums in the center. Roll out the second ball to the same thickness and place it over the plums. Crimp the edges of the crusts together with a fork. With a sharp knife, cut six 1-inch vents in the top crust to allow steam to escape. Brush the top crust with cold water and sprinkle with the remaining sugar.
4. Bake until the pastry is golden brown, 30 to 40 minutes.
5. Remove from the oven and let cool slightly. Brush the top with the reduced plum juice and serve warm.

★ If you make the
tart the same day, let
the lemons cool in
their water, uncov-
ered. Refrigerate the
pastry for 1 to 2
hours before rolling
it out, then for at
least 1 hour in the
tart pan before
filling.

Ginger Lemon Tart

Makes one 9-inch tart; 6 to 8 servings

This is a truly elegant dessert, and one that is different from your usual neon yellow custard-filled lemon tart. It combines the flavors of ginger, brown sugar, and lemon, giving it a rich caramel color while retaining a light taste. I like to use the Cream Cheese Pastry, which can be made the day before and rolled out the day you bake the tart. The filling and the lemon slices can be prepared up to two days in advance, so you have only the assembly to do at the last minute.

1 cup water

2 lemons, thinly sliced and seeded

2 tablespoons granulated sugar

½ recipe Cream Cheese Pastry
   (recipe follows)

4 large eggs, at room temperature

3 tablespoons heavy cream

1 teaspoon pure vanilla extract

Pinch of salt

¼ cup crystallized ginger

2 tablespoons grated lemon rind

1 cup firmly packed light brown sugar

½ cup (1 stick) unsalted butter, melted

1. In a medium-size nonreactive saucepan, bring the water to a boil. Add the lemon slices and granulated sugar and stir until the sugar dissolves. Reduce the heat to low and simmer for 5 minutes. The lemons can be stored in their cooking water, covered tightly with plastic wrap, for up to 2 days in the refrigerator. Let them come to room temperature before using. When ready to use, discard the water and set the lemon slices aside on a plate.

2. On a lightly floured board, roll the pastry out into a circle about ½ inch thick. Fit it into a 9-inch pie plate or tart pan. Shape the edge so that it is slightly higher than the pan, then cover with plastic wrap and refrigerate for at least 1 hour.

3. Preheat the oven to 350°F.

4. Place the eggs, cream, vanilla, salt, ginger, lemon rind, and brown sugar in a food processor and pulse, then process, until smooth. With the machine running, add the melted butter slowly until everything is mixed well. Pour the custard into the chilled crust and bake until the custard is set and the crust is golden brown, 40 to 50 minutes.

5. Let the tart cool completely, then decorate the top with the softened lemon slices. Refrigerate for at least 2 hours before serving.

Cream Cheese Pastry   *Makes two 9-inch crusts*

My friend Monique made this wonderful crust when we cooked with James Beard more than 30 years ago. We entertained a great deal in those days and did it all ourselves. This recipe is easy, and I use it often. I can still picture Monique's hands making the soft dough.

1 cup (2 sticks) unsalted butter,
    softened
One 8-ounce package cream cheese,
    softened

2 cups all-purpose flour
½ teaspoon salt

Place the butter and cream cheese in a food processor and pulse until well combined. Add the flour and salt and pulse again until the dough forms a ball. Divide into 2 even-size balls and cover tightly with plastic wrap. Refrigerate for at least 1 hour or overnight before using as instructed in the specific recipe.

Last-Minute Dinner with Friends

Using What's in the Pantry

Broiled Sesame Cheesies

Pasta Puttanesca

Crispy Romaine Salad

Bread and Butter Pudding

It is not often, thank goodness, but it has happened that my husband calls up and says, "Honey, would you mind if I brought a few people home for dinner tonight?" Sometimes I get a message on the machine with that request, always with the sendoff, "Something really easy . . . don't fuss." I never panic in these situations because I have the ingredients for a quick and delicious menu in my kitchen cabinet. I call this my larder, as many people do, and on page xvii I list my must-have ingredients for emergencies. I may have to run out for a head of lettuce or a fresh loaf of bread, but the basics are there. The pasta sauce here is built

around garlic, olive oil, black olives, tomatoes, capers, and anchovies. The Bread and Butter Pudding is silky custard inside and crunchy, sugary bread on top. It's hard to beat that finish to a meal.

When I have chosen a simple pasta dinner like this one, I like to make the table look a little special. An easy centerpiece is a collection of beautiful geraniums, still in their perfect green pots. I use a hand-embroidered "Home, sweet home" tablecloth and matching napkins that I got in the '60s. Your guests will be amazed that you took the time to cook for them on such short notice.

Broiled Sesame Cheesies

Makes 8 servings

I first had this at my daughter Lexie's house very recently—she is a good cook but busy with her job and her two cute little girls. This crispy little buttery triangle toasted with sesame seeds goes with soups and salads. It is a versatile accompaniment to almost any meal. Kids love these as well.

4 pita breads

¼ cup (½ stick) butter, softened

½ cup shredded Monterey Jack cheese

2 tablespoons sesame seeds

1. Preheat the oven to 300°F.
2. Split the pita breads. Spread the butter on the inside and sprinkle with the grated cheese and sesame seeds. Cut into triangles, place on ungreased cookie sheets, and bake until golden brown, 7 to 8 minutes.
3. Serve warm in a basket lined with a large, pretty napkin.

ELLEN'S TIPS

★ Instead of sesame seeds, you can use poppy seeds, caraway seeds, black mustard seeds, or cumin seeds. Or try an herb such as chopped fresh parsley leaves, cilantro leaves, or chives, to name just a few.

Pasta Puttanesca

Makes 6 to 8 servings

The literal translation of puttanesca is "whore's sauce." The name refers to the sauce's earthiness and robust flavor and the fact that it can be put together very quickly—in between appointments. I learned the recipe from my old friend Ben Gazzara, the actor, who many years ago taught me his Italian spin on cooking pasta. He is a very good cook who loves to eat, and this is one recipe I make time after time because of its unusual taste. I make sure always to have these ingredients on hand. Perciatelli is a thick spaghetti with a hole in the center that is becoming increasingly available.

3 tablespoons olive oil

6 to 8 cloves garlic, to your taste, crushed

Two 2-ounce tins flat anchovies, drained

6 cups canned crushed tomatoes

½ cup capers, drained

1 cup pitted black olives, drained and quartered

½ cup water

2 or 3 hot cherry peppers, to your taste, rinsed

1 teaspoon vegetable or olive oil

1 teaspoon salt

2 pounds perciatelli or thick spaghetti

1. In a medium-size saucepan over medium heat, heat the olive oil. Add the garlic and cook, stirring, until lightly browned, about 2 minutes. Add the anchovies and stir until they melt into the oil. Add the tomatoes, capers, olives, water, and cherry peppers. Cover and simmer for 30 minutes.

2. With a slotted spoon, remove the peppers from the sauce. Remove the stems and chop the peppers. Place them in a tiny serving bowl and add 2 tablespoons of the sauce. Set aside, then serve with a small spoon for those fans of hot-and-spicy.

3. Bring a large pot of water to a boil and add the vegetable oil and salt. Cook the

ELLEN'S TIPS

★ Any kind of pitted black olives are good.

★ This sauce also works well with other pasta shapes, such as rigatoni and fusilli.

★ Never put cheese on top of pasta with fish in it. Italians disapprove!

★ I put a teaspoon of leftover sauce on tomato slices. It's great cold!

pasta until *al dente*, about 10 minutes. Drain, then return the pasta to the pot and cover until you are ready to serve.

4. When ready to serve, put the pasta and a ladleful of the sauce in a large serving bowl. Toss lightly, then serve with more sauce on each portion. Serve the hot sauce on the side.

Crispy Romaine Salad

Makes 8 servings

ELLEN'S TIPS

★ You cannot refrigerate cut and cleaned salad makings for longer than 2 hours. After that, the lettuce begins to wilt and lose its crispness.

★ Do not drown the salad with dressing. This is one place where more is not better.

★ I suggest basil, but oregano also works well.

Romaine lettuce is the crunchiest lettuce of all, and when you use the younger leaves, it's the best. It's a perfect foil to the spice of the pasta sauce.

1 head romaine lettuce, tender heart only, washed, dried, and cut into bite-size pieces

1 medium-size cucumber, peeled and sliced

6 or 7 radishes, peeled and cut into small chunks

1 teaspoon dried basil

½ cup Ellen's Favorite Dressing: Version 1 (page 110)

1. Put the lettuce in a large salad bowl. Arrange the cucumber and radishes on top. Sprinkle with the basil. Cover with a clean kitchen towel and refrigerate until ready to serve.
2. Just before serving, pour on the dressing and toss well to coat evenly.

Bread and Butter Pudding

Makes 8 to 10 servings

This recipe is one of my favorites and was one of James Beard's as well. It was originally from an old New York restaurant called the Coach House, which is long gone. It is part pudding and part candy, creamy and crunchy all at the same time. It can be made in the morning, set aside, and served after running it quickly under the broiler.

Eight to ten ½-inch-thick slices French or Italian bread, cut at a sharp angle

¼ cup (½ stick) unsalted butter, softened

5 large eggs, at room temperature

4 large egg yolks, at room temperature

1 cup granulated sugar

⅛ teaspoon salt

4 cups whole milk

1 cup heavy cream

One 12-inch-long vanilla bean, split lengthwise, or 1 teaspoon pure vanilla extract

½ cup confectioners' sugar

1 cup heavy cream, for serving

1. Preheat the oven to 375°F. Butter a 2-quart baking dish.
2. Trim the crusts off the bread, butter each slice generously on one side, and set aside.
3. In a large mixing bowl, beat the eggs, egg yolks, granulated sugar, and salt until thoroughly blended.
4. Place the milk and cream in a medium-size saucepan over high heat. Add the vanilla bean, if using, and heat until bubbles form around the edge of the pan. This process is called scalding. Don't let the mixture come to a boil. Remove the vanilla bean and scrape the little seeds inside back into the milk mixture. Discard the husk. If you are using vanilla extract, stir that in now. Gradually stir the milk mixture into the egg mixture, spoonful by spoonful. Do not use an electric mixer to do this.

5. Overlap the bread, butter side up, in the prepared baking dish and pour the milk-egg mixture through a fine-mesh strainer over the bread. Set the baking dish in a larger pan with enough hot water to come halfway up the dish; this is known as a water bath, or *bain-marie*. Bake until the bread is golden brown, about 45 minutes.

6. When ready to serve, sprinkle generously with the confectioners' sugar and place under the broiler at close range until browned, 20 to 30 seconds. Watch it the entire time; it can burn in a flash.

7. Pour the heavy cream into a pitcher and serve with the pudding.

ELLEN'S TIPS

★ Using a vanilla bean is preferable to using extract. It requires just a bit of extra time, but the flavor is worth it.

Nana and Papa Joe's "Silly Supper"

When the Parents Are Away and We're in Charge

Homemade Tortilla Chips and Sour Cream
  Clam Dip

Franks and Beans Casserole

French Fries

My Favorite Coleslaw

Make-Your-Own Sundaes with Nana's Hot Fudge Sauce

Every once in a while, we get lucky. Our children allow us the privilege of taking our grandchildren by ourselves, without their supervision, inexperienced as we may be. They leave us pages of instructions, 5 to 10 emergency phone numbers, and specific parenting tips. Then we get to take over for the weekend, the day, or even just an afternoon. We relish the opportunity to be together, to bend (or break) the rules, to eat at "funny" times, and just to enjoy each other.

This meal is prepared and eaten on the deck or in the kitchen, depending on weather, and it is a great opportunity to get your grandchildren, whatever their ages, to take part. They love to measure and pour, toss the coleslaw, and set the table. Just to be silly, we sometimes wear wild and crazy hats while we eat. The kids have their own assignments, such as gathering ingredients, pulling out equipment, and measuring. The sundaes are fun for all of us. I put out little custard cups filled with nuts, chocolate bits, mini marsh-mallows, and jimmies (or sprinkles, if you didn't grow up in Massachusetts). We all help to make this the most fun possible, and Papa Joe and I get a little bit kooky for the occasion.

Homemade Tortilla Chips and
Sour Cream Clam Dip

Makes 8 servings

I love making these chips myself because they are head and shoulders above the store-bought ones. It sounds like a lot of work, but it isn't. All you do is cut soft corn tortillas into quarters, brush them with canola oil, and bake slowly until they harden and brown. Add a little salt, and you're done. Embarrassingly easy but amazingly good.

Six to eight 6-inch soft corn tortillas

2 tablespoons canola oil

One 4-ounce can chopped clams

2 cups sour cream

½ envelope dry onion soup mix

1. Preheat the oven to 300°F.
2. Cut each tortilla into quarters to form 4 triangles. Brush with the canola oil and place on cookie sheets. Bake until crisp, 30 to 40 minutes. Remove from the oven and let cool on the sheets.
3. Drain the clams thoroughly. In a medium-size mixing bowl, combine them with the sour cream and onion soup mix.
4. Serve the chips on a pretty round platter or in a basket, with the dip in a small bowl in the center.

Franks and Beans Casserole

Makes 8 servings

This makes a great quick lunch or supper when you don't want a lot of work. The taste of brown sugar and bacon with the franks sort of dresses up this grand old favorite. My choice is the fat knockwurst-type frank, although any good-quality all-beef frank will work fine.

Two 16-ounce cans baked beans
8 to 10 knockwurst or 10 to 12
   all-beef franks

½ cup firmly packed dark
   brown sugar
4 strips bacon

1. Preheat the oven to 350°F.
2. Place the beans in a 2-quart baking dish. Press the franks down into the beans. I leave them whole, but some people like to cut them into pieces on the diagonal. Sprinkle ¼ cup of the brown sugar evenly over the top. Lay the bacon strips on top and sprinkle with the remaining ¼ cup brown sugar.
3. Bake until the bacon is crisp and the beans are bubbly, 30 to 45 minutes.

ELLEN'S TIPS

★ I like to use plain baked beans, without added ketchup or onions.

★ The usual condiments—pickles, mustard, ketchup, chips, and sliced onion—go well with this meal.

★ The casserole can get overcooked and dry if you leave it in the oven too long. Be watchful.

French Fries

Makes 6 to 8 servings

Homemade French fries are so easy to make and always worth the effort. The key is hot oil and cold potatoes.

3 large Idaho potatoes
3 cups canola oil

Kosher salt to taste

1. Preheat the oven to 200°F.
2. Peel and slice the potatoes into French fry–size strips and drop in cold water to keep them white.
3. In a large, deep skillet over medium-high heat, heat the oil until it is very hot but not smoking. Drop in batches of potatoes (be careful not to crowd them) and cook until golden brown, 4 to 5 minutes. Using a slotted spoon, transfer to paper towels to drain. Continue until all the fries are cooked. Keep warm in the oven.
4. Let cool a little, sprinkle with salt, and serve in a basket lined with a pretty napkin.

ELLEN'S TIPS

★ I test the heat of the oil by letting a drop of water fall into it. If it makes a spitting noise, it's hot enough.

★ Only keep warm for 30 to 40 minutes or these will get soggy.

My Favorite Coleslaw

Makes 8 servings

I have been making this coleslaw since 1972, when my children were young. Served cold and crisp, it can't be beat. Pass it alongside substantial main dishes such as meat loaf, short ribs, or chops.

1 large head white cabbage, cored

Dressing:
½ cup olive oil
3 tablespoons red wine vinegar
1 teaspoon salt
½ teaspoon freshly ground
    black pepper

1 teaspoon celery seeds
1 teaspoon mustard seeds
1 teaspoon sugar
½ teaspoon dry mustard
¾ cup mayonnaise

1. Slice the cabbage thinly and set aside in a large mixing bowl.
2. To make the dressing, whisk together all the ingredients in a medium-size mixing bowl. Pour half of it over the sliced cabbage and toss well to distribute. Depending on the size of the head of cabbage you are using, you can add the rest of the dressing or reserve some, so that the cabbage is coated but not swimming in dressing. Cover with plastic wrap and refrigerate for 3 to 4 hours before serving.

ELLEN'S TIPS

★ This recipe *must* be made the day you're going to serve it. It gets soggy after sitting overnight.

★ The secret to better coleslaw is to cut the cabbage thin, thin, thin.

★ This dressing tastes equally yummy on sliced cucumbers.

★ Be sure to have
glasses of ice water
ready for a sundae
accompaniment.

Make-Your-Own Sundaes with
Nana's Hot Fudge Sauce

Makes 8 servings

Everyone loves ice cream and especially if you get to put all kinds of stuff on it. The best part of this dessert is my homemade fudge sauce. You can be creative and eat as much as you want, especially if the parents aren't looking.

2 quarts vanilla ice cream
3 cups Nana's Hot Fudge Sauce
   (recipe follows)
1 cup chopped walnuts
1 cup Marshmallow Fluff,
   heated

Small bowls of any or all of the
   following: rainbow or chocolate
   sprinkles, semisweet chocolate bits,
   mini marshmallows, M&M's,
   crushed Oreo or chocolate chip
   cookies
Maraschino cherries (optional)

Put a scoop of ice cream in a pretty dish for each person and let everyone help themselves to the toppings.

Nana's Hot Fudge Sauce

Makes 2 cups

I got this recipe from my pastry teacher, Maurice Bonte. He had a little pastry shop on Third Avenue and taught an extensive course in pastry in James Beard's kitchen many years ago.

6 ounces unsweetened chocolate
1 cup half-and-half

1½ cups sugar
1 teaspoon pure vanilla extract

1. Put the chocolate, half-and-half, sugar, and vanilla in a medium-size microwave-safe bowl or measuring cup. Heat in the microwave on medium power for 2 to 3 minutes. When the chocolate is fully melted, beat with a spoon until smooth.

2. You can store the sauce in a jar for up to 1 week in the refrigerator. Reheat it in the microwave for 30 seconds.

ELLEN'S TIPS

★ To reheat the sauce on the stovetop, place the jar, uncovered, in a saucepan of simmering water and heat through, 3 to 4 minutes, stirring a few times.

My Daughter's in the Kitchen

Step Aside, Mom

Cold Senegalese Soup

Baked Cod with Tomato Herb Salsa

Sugar Snap Peas

Monkey Bread

Summer Pudding

All my children are good cooks, but Claudia, my eldest, entertains the most. She reminds me of myself when I was her age. She has three small children, but she is not afraid to cook for a crowd. She loves planning and organizing the meal and dressing up the table with special treats, always color coordinated, and she likes company. I am happy to chop and do whatever she needs, like a good sous chef. The table is set with a collection of striped napkins in many colors and a matching checkered tablecloth. Serving the wine in multicolored Moroccan tea glasses with gold etching is a fun addition to the meal.

Enormous wine goblets hold the curried soup that starts the ball rolling. The bright green sugar snap peas look wonderful with the fish. The chopped red salsa, served in my grandson Jonny's "knee" bowl—made out of the clay impression of his knee and painted by Jonny himself—adds a conversation piece to the setting. But I think the Monkey Bread is the best surprise of all. Individual cups of summer pudding with red and blue berries and whipped cream finish this summer meal with a bang.

Cold Senegalese Soup

Makes 6 to 8 servings

When I lived in Florida in the early 1990s, my daughters Claudia and Lexie loved to eat this soup. Whenever they would visit, we would treat ourselves to a decadent mother-daughter lunch at a place called Café Europa in Palm Beach, where we would enjoy cold curried cream of chicken soup served in a giant wine goblet, along with a glass of champagne. If you want a summer menu that is refreshing and tasty, serve this along with bread sticks and salad as a meal. It has pieces of tender chicken and crisp chopped apple, resulting in a lively balance of tastes and textures. When serving it as a first course, I omit the chicken.

6 leeks

4 or 5 medium-size all-purpose
   potatoes

3 green apples, such as Pippin,
   Granny Smith, or Golden Delicious

Juice of ½ lemon

¼ cup (½ stick) butter

¾ cup finely chopped onion

½ teaspoon finely chopped garlic

2 tablespoons freshly purchased mild
   curry powder

6 cups strong chicken broth
   (see Ellen's Tips)

1 cup heavy cream

Freshly ground white pepper to taste

1 whole chicken breast, gently poached
   (see Ellen's Tips), bones and skin
   discarded, meat shredded

1. Trim the leeks and soak them in cold water to rid them of any sand. Slice the white parts only. You will have about 2½ cups. Peel the potatoes, then cut them into 1-inch cubes. Place in a medium-size bowl with cold water to cover. Peel and core the apples, then cut them into ½-inch cubes. Place in a medium-size bowl with cold water to cover. Add the lemon juice to keep them from turning brown. When ready to begin, drain everything except half the apples.

2. In a large saucepan over medium-high heat, melt the butter. Reduce the heat to medium, add the leeks, onion, garlic, and half the apples. Cook, stirring, until tender, 4 to 5 minutes. Stir in the curry powder and cook, stirring, for 2 minutes.

★ To make a stronger broth, add 2 chicken bouillon cubes to your regular broth.

★ If the soup is too thick, thin it with chicken stock or a little cream. It should be the consistency of heavy cream.

★ Use chicken with the bones and skin—it has more flavor. To poach, put the breast in a deep skillet over low heat and add water to cover. Simmer, covered, until no longer pink, 10 to 15 minutes.

Add the potatoes and chicken broth, cover, and simmer until the potatoes are tender, about 45 minutes. Stir in the cream.

3. Remove from the heat and let cool. Transfer to a food processor or a blender in batches and process until smooth. Add the pepper and stir to combine. Transfer to a large bowl, cover with plastic, and refrigerate for at least 4 hours or overnight.

4. Serve in chilled wine goblets, cups, or bowls, garnished with the shredded chicken and remaining chopped apples.

Baked Cod with Tomato Herb Salsa

Makes 6 to 8 servings

I used to make this dish with Chilean sea bass, but since it has become overfished and is now on the endangered species list, I wouldn't think of buying it. The recipe is just as good with cod, scrod, halibut, or any other white, flaky fish. The herbed topping is one of my daughter Claudia's recipes. She throws this dish together at the drop of a hat.

6 to 8 thick cod fillets

3 tablespoons olive oil

2 medium-size ripe tomatoes, chopped

4 large cloves garlic, chopped

1 tablespoon fresh lemon juice

1 teaspoon chopped fresh chervil leaves

1 tablespoon chopped fresh parsley leaves

1 teaspoon chopped fresh marjoram leaves

2 lemons, quartered, for garnish

1. Preheat the oven to 450°F. Lightly oil a large baking dish.
2. Wash the fillets and pat dry with paper towels. Arrange in a single layer in the prepared baking dish. Brush with some of the olive oil and bake until the thickest part of the fillets flakes when pulled on with a fork, about 30 minutes.
3. In a medium-size mixing bowl, combine the tomatoes, garlic, lemon juice, and remaining olive oil and toss to coat the tomatoes.
4. In a small bowl, combine the herbs, which will be used at the last minute.
5. When the fish is done, transfer to a pretty platter. Garnish each piece with a generous spoonful of the tomato mixture and sprinkle with the mixed herbs. Decorate with the lemon wedges.

ELLEN'S TIPS

★ One-half pound of fish per person is the right amount, although that is a bit too much for a small eater. Still, I find that I never have any left over because the big eaters always end up eating what the little eaters don't.

★ You can use any herbs you like. I have used fresh cilantro, thyme, oregano, dill, and sage with good results. Parsley is the one thing that you need to bring them all together. Limit the number of herbs to 3.

Sugar Snap Peas

Makes 8 servings

There is nothing more gorgeous and bright, clear green than sugar snap peas cooked quickly this way. They add so much to a meal.

2 pounds sugar snap peas
¼ cup (½ stick) butter

1. Clean the peas by pinching off the ends and pulling the strings if they come off naturally. The young ones don't need this.
2. Melt the butter in a large skillet over medium-high heat. Add the peas and cook, shaking the pan constantly, until they turn bright green, 3 to 5 minutes.
3. Serve warm as soon as possible.

Monkey Bread

Makes 6 servings

This recipe was quite popular in the 1960s and 1970s, and I believe it is making a comeback. It is too simple for words—great for the kids to help make. And everyone, old and young, loves to pull off one buttery roll after another and eat it, just like a happy monkey.

2 to 3 tubes prepared dinner rolls
or croissants

½ cup (1 stick) butter, melted

1. Preheat the oven to 350°F.
2. Dip each roll in the melted butter and stack them in a 2-quart tube or bundt pan on top of each other, leaving 2 inches at the top. Bake until the rolls puff up and turn golden brown, 45 to 55 minutes.
3. Let cool slightly and unmold onto a pretty plate. Put in the center of the table and have guests tear off the rolls as desired.

ELLEN'S TIPS

★ You may steam the peas, if you wish, over a pot with about an inch of boiling water and a bit of salt. It should take about 3 minutes, but be careful because it's easy to overcook them.

★ Try adding some chopped fresh parsley leaves right before serving.

★ You can combine dinner rolls and croissants to vary the layers of rolls. Any kind of ready-to-bake roll is good for this recipe.

★ If you have a larger bundt pan or mold, use an extra tube of rolls. Bake 10 to 20 minutes longer.

Summer Pudding

Makes 6 to 8 servings

I was at a dinner in the English countryside one June several years ago, and summer pudding was served. I almost turned it down, until the beautiful elderly woman sitting next to me said, "Oh, you must try it. I wait all year for this dessert, and you will love it, I am sure!" She couldn't have been more correct. It was wonderful beyond words. You, too, must try it. It has to be made the day before.

1 pint small strawberries, hulled
¾ cup sugar
1½ pints raspberries, picked over
½ pint blackberries, picked over
1 pint blueberries, picked over
2 tablespoons fresh lemon juice

Pinch of salt
18 slices white bread, crusts trimmed
    and bread cut into 4- to 5-inch
    circles
1 pint heavy cream, whipped to
    soft peaks, for serving

1. In a large nonreactive saucepan over medium heat, cook the strawberries and sugar for 5 minutes, stirring frequently. Add the rest of the berries and cook for 5 minutes more, stirring gently from time to time. Transfer to a large mixing bowl and stir in the lemon juice and salt.

2. Line 6 to 8 custard cups or small ramekins with plastic wrap—enough to cover the inside of the cup with a little to drape over the edge. Spoon 2 tablespoons of the berry mixture into each cup. Dip a circle of bread in berry juice and fit that into the

★ Never wash raspberries or black-berries; they are too fragile and absorbent and become mushy when doused with water. Strawberries must be washed. Blueberries need only to be picked over for leaves and stems.

★ If you overcook the fruit, it will be-come mush. You want the berries to keep their shapes a bit.

★ Fill the custard cups above the top so that when they are weighted down, they will compress and unmold better.

★ You cannot unmold the puddings a day ahead because they may not keep their shape.

cup. Add another 2 tablespoons berry mixture and top with another berry juice–soaked bread circle. The cups should be quite full.

3. Place the custard cups in a large baking pan and cover with a large piece of plastic wrap. Weight the cups with a cutting board or something else large and flat. Then add some extra weights, such as tomato cans, a brick, or a heavy teakettle with water in it. Refrigerate overnight.

4. When ready to serve, unmold the custard cups onto serving plates and serve each with a dollop of whipped cream.

Private Date for Two
Sharing Secrets

My Gazpacho

Sublime Cheese Soufflé

The Best Watercress Salad

Nettie's Chocolate Chip Cake
   with Quick Chocolate Frosting

When my children were in grade school, one of their favorite treats was a private date with me. We would go to our neighborhood coffee shop and sit in a booth, sharing a toasted corn muffin and hot chocolate. They have all said these were among the most memorable times we spent together. Children need that time to relax and ask questions. And they love not having to share you with anyone else. They will talk like grownups and tell you everything.

I love making this soufflé menu for a child or grandchild. If you have a long private date, he or she can help you make it. James Beard always told me that the best way to learn to fold egg whites is with your hands. Children love that. I always have some small surprise at the table, such as a heart-shaped Barbie notebook and special pen for one of my sweet granddaughters.

My Gazpacho

Serves 4 with extra

ELLEN'S TIPS

★ The way to stretch this soup and make more is by adding more tomato juice and chopped vegetables.

Gazpacho recipes have gone through many incarnations. This one has truly grown through the years. I like to serve it in small mugs for my little guests to accompany this cheese soufflé because the combination is so good. In the summer I keep it in a pitcher in the fridge so people can help themselves.

4 radishes, trimmed and chopped

1 small red onion

1 rib celery, trimmed

1 small cucumber, peeled, seeded, and cubed

1 medium-size carrot, trimmed

⅓ cup peeled and diced jicama

1 tablespoon Worcestershire sauce

White pepper to taste

¼ teaspoon celery salt

½ cup beef broth (canned is fine)

3 cups tomato juice

Juice of ½ lemon

Tabasco sauce to taste (for the adults)

4 ribs celery, trimmed, for decoration

Take all the vegetables and chop them coarsely in batches in the food processor. Do not puree them. Add the seasonings, beef broth, and tomato and lemon juices. Taste as you go along so that you get what you like. Chill for at least 2 hours. Serve with a stick of celery.

Sublime Cheese Soufflé

Makes 2 servings

Don't let the word soufflé put you off. This is easy to make and ideal for an intimate light dinner or lunch. It is indeed sublime—the way it rises and is so cloudlike—almost ethereal.

5 level tablespoons all-purpose flour

1 cup cold milk

Freshly grated nutmeg to taste

Salt and freshly ground black pepper
   to taste

3 large egg yolks, at room temperature

4 large egg whites, at room
   temperature

½ cup shredded Swiss cheese (I like
   Jarlsberg)

1. Preheat the oven to 375°F. Butter a 10-inch soufflé dish and put it in the refrigerator. Place a large pan with 1 inch of hot water on the center oven rack. This is called a *bain-marie*, or water bath, and will help the soufflé cook gently and evenly.

2. Put the flour in a large, heavy saucepan over medium heat. Pour the milk bit by bit into the flour, beating well with a whisk after each addition. Season with the nutmeg and salt and pepper. Cook, stirring constantly, until thickened, 4 to 5 minutes. You may need to reduce the heat to keep the mixture from thickening too fast. Add the egg yolks one at a time, beating well with a wooden spoon after each addition. Remove from the heat and let cool until you can put your finger in comfortably.

3. In a large mixing bowl with an electric mixer at high speed, beat the egg whites until they hold stiff peaks when the beater is raised. Fold into the milk mixture, then fold in the cheese. Transfer to the soufflé dish. Place the dish in the water bath and bake in the exact center of the oven until it turns golden brown, about 40 minutes. Don't open the oven door for at least 30 minutes while the soufflé is baking.

4. Bring the soufflé to the table immediately for your dinner partner to admire, then serve.

(continued on page 205)

ELLEN'S TIPS

★ The eggs *must* be at room temperature for this dish, as warm whites whip to a much greater volume than cold ones. Take them out of the refrigerator about 1 hour before you are going to whip them.

★ When serving a soufflé, I usually have everything else ready at the table. The iced tea or lemonade is poured, water is in the glasses, and my little guest is seated when I remove the soufflé from the oven.

Timesaving Tip

Here's another way to divide the work.

1. Cook the flour, milk, and egg yolk mixture. Cover the pan and remove from the heat. Reheat slightly when you are ready to assemble the soufflé.

2. About 45 minutes before you want to eat, beat the egg whites until stiff peaks form.

3. When you're ready for the soufflé, fold the shredded cheese into the egg whites, then fold the egg whites into the warm egg yolk mixture. Proceed as directed.

The Best Watercress Salad

Makes 2 servings

ELLEN'S TIPS

(continued from page 203)

★ "Folding" should be done with a large rubber spatula using a U-shaped motion. That way, a lot of air is incorporated into the soufflé to give it maximum volume.

I love the freshness of watercress, which combines well with other lettuces, especially Belgian endive. Add a simple dressing, and you have something special.

1 bunch watercress

1 small Belgian endive

¼ cup Ellen's Favorite Dressing: Version 1 (page 110)

1. Wash the watercress and spin dry. Break off the large stems and place the tender watercress in a salad bowl.
2. Core, split, and slice the endive. Add to the bowl. Cover with a clean dishtowel and refrigerate.
3. When ready to serve, toss the greens evenly with the dressing.

Nettie's Chocolate Chip Cake with Quick Chocolate Frosting

Makes one 8-inch cake

When I was age 20, I met an older woman named Nettie. She was a baby nurse for a friend of mine, and she loved to bake. I lived in San Francisco at the time. I tasted her cake and loved it, but when I asked her for the recipe, she said it was only in her head. She did let me watch her as she threw together a little of this and a little of that until it felt right to her. I wrote down the recipe as best I could capture it. I have kept it for more than 40 years, and everyone still loves it. Chocolate or white frosting works very nicely with it. Even just a dusting of confectioners' sugar is fine. This cake is so delicious that it's worth making for any special occasion, especially for children.

1 cup (2 sticks) unsalted butter, softened
1 cup granulated sugar
½ cup firmly packed light or dark brown sugar
2 large eggs, at room temperature
1 cup sour cream
2 cups all-purpose flour, sifted
½ teaspoon baking soda

1 teaspoon baking powder
Pinch of ground mace
1 teaspoon ground cinnamon
2 tablespoons whole milk
1 cup chopped walnuts
½ cup semisweet chocolate bits
Quick Chocolate Frosting
  (recipe follows)

1. Preheat the oven to 350°F. Butter and flour an 8-inch square baking pan, knocking out the excess flour.
2. In a large mixing bowl with an electric mixer on medium speed, cream together the butter and sugars until smooth. Add the eggs one at a time, beating well after each addition. Add the sour cream and mix well.
3. In a medium-size mixing bowl, combine the flour, baking soda, baking powder, mace, and cinnamon. Add to the butter mixture and mix on low speed. Add the milk and beat well.

4. Add the nuts and chocolate bits and stir with a wooden spoon until well distributed.

5. Pour the batter into the prepared pan. Bake until the sides begin to pull away from the pan and a cake tester inserted in the center comes out clean, 30 to 40 minutes.

6. When cool to the touch, about 10 minutes, ice with the frosting.

Quick Chocolate Frosting   *Makes 2 cups*

This frosting is a formula for success: quick and good. Keep these ingredients on hand, and you'll always be ready to frost a cake.

½ cup (1 stick) unsalted butter, softened

One 16-ounce package confectioners' sugar

1 teaspoon pure vanilla extract

3 tablespoons unsweetened cocoa powder

3 to 4 tablespoons heavy cream, light cream, or whole milk, as needed

In a medium-size mixing bowl, beat the butter and confectioners' sugar with a wooden spoon until smooth. Add the vanilla, cocoa, and half the cream and stir until the frosting has the consistency of mayonnaise. Add more cream if it is too thick. If refrigerated, it will thicken and become more difficult to spread, so it's better to use it right away.

ELLEN'S TIPS

★ You can moisten the frosting with a little coffee if you want a mocha taste.

★ The reason for no electric mixer is that the frosting becomes too fluffy and tastes less chocolatey. It's not bad, but the color and texture is different.

★ If you add the liquid too quickly, the frosting may get too thin, so be careful to add it little by little.

After a Long Weekend with Guests

Too Tired to Cook

Cherry Tomatoes with Sea Salt

Golden Flounder

Warm Beet Salad with Iceberg
   Lettuce Wedges

Rice Pudding

Sliced Summer Peaches and Cream

I never know exactly what I can get away with after a busy weekend with guests at the beach. Should we go out? Should we order for take-out? Should we stop for a pizza on the way back into the city and call it a day? If I were alone, I would have a bowl of Cream of Wheat with sugar and milk and go to bed. But if I give it some thought, I stop and buy some fresh fish at one of the many no-name shacks at the beach. I have them pack it in ice and keep it in my small cooler. This meal is perfect for all my needs because the fish takes no time and looks great. I bring beets back to the city from my garden, along with tomatoes and peaches from the farm stand. The Roquefort cheese and iceberg lettuce are already in my fridge. Sometimes I have leftover rice pudding and use it to go along with my peaches and cream. It's a relief to end with a meal that isn't too much work, and I feel proud of myself for having made the weekend last a little longer with a taste of the beach brought back to the city.

Cherry Tomatoes with Sea Salt

Makes 6 servings

What is better than fresh-from-the-garden cherry tomatoes sprinkled with sea salt? When the good ones are in season, we can eat right from the vine.

1 box sweet cherry tomatoes
1 tablespoon sea salt or kosher salt

Wash the tomatoes and slightly dry them. Place in a lovely bowl, preferably glass, and toss with the salt.

Golden Flounder

Makes 6 to 8 servings

ELLEN'S TIPS

★ You can decorate the fish with chopped fresh parsley leaves or chives and lemon wedges, which looks especially pretty on a white platter.

This easy and tasty recipe is from my kids. Yes, once again, Mom is learning from her children—all the time. Lexie and Bill make this dish at home. We have all learned how to make it, and it's a snap. It is crunchy and buttery and so simple, made with the freshest of fish, crushed saltine crackers, and melted butter. We can all share this one. My son-in-law Bill is my resident wine connoisseur, so I count on his help in that department.

6 to 7 very fresh flounder, sole, or cod fillets (about ½ pound each)
1 tablespoon fresh lemon juice

1 sleeve saltine crackers, coarsely crushed (1 cup)
½ cup (1 stick) butter, melted

1. Preheat the oven to 350°F. Butter a 9 x 13-inch baking dish.
2. Wash the fillets in cold water and pat dry with paper towels. Arrange the fillets in a single layer in the prepared dish. Sprinkle with the lemon juice. Cover the fish evenly with the crushed crackers and drizzle with the butter.
3. Bake until browned, about 30 minutes. Serve immediately.

Warm Beet Salad with Iceberg Lettuce Wedges

Makes 8 servings

ELLEN'S TIPS

★ Scallions or red onions can be substituted for chives.

★ You can substitute any lettuce here, such as romaine, endive, or Boston.

For beet lovers like me, this salad is simple, pure, and wonderful. If you can get yellow and red beets, you can mix them, and the result is just beautiful. All one color is very nice, too. I serve them with iceberg lettuce wedges, creamy vinaigrette, and crumbled bacon and blue cheese. The combination of warm beets and cool lettuce is perfect for a summer night.

2 bunches yellow or red beets, or a combination

1 tablespoon butter, softened

Salt and freshly ground black pepper to taste

½ cup sour cream

1 cup Ellen's Favorite Dressing: Version 1 (page 110)

1 head iceberg lettuce, cored and cut into wedges

4 tablespoons crumbled blue cheese

6 strips bacon, cooked until crisp, drained on paper towels, and crumbled, for garnish

Chopped fresh chives (optional), for garnish

1. Wash the beets and discard the greens. Place the beets in a medium-size saucepan with water to cover by 2 inches. Cover and cook over medium heat until the beets can be pierced easily with a knife, about 30 minutes. Drain.

2. Under cool running water, peel the beets by sticking a long-tined fork into the stem end and scraping the skin away with a knife. Trim, slice, or quarter the beets and place them in a large bowl. Add the butter and toss to coat. Cover and keep warm until ready to serve. Just before serving, sprinkle with salt and pepper.

3. In a small mixing bowl, whip together the sour cream and dressing.

4. To serve, arrange the beets and lettuce wedges attractively on a serving plate and sprinkle with the blue cheese. Pour some of the dressing over the lettuce and garnish the beets and lettuce with the bacon and the chives, if using. Serve the remaining dressing in a small pitcher at the table.

Rice Pudding

Makes 6 servings

I like to serve rice pudding with peaches, sugar, and cream, although it's also great just by itself.

1 tablespoon butter

2 tablespoons plain dry bread crumbs

2 cups cooked long-grain white rice

1 cup whole milk

1 cup light or heavy cream

⅛ teaspoon salt

⅓ cup sugar

2 teaspoons pure vanilla extract

2 large eggs, at room temperature, well beaten

¼ cup golden raisins (optional)

1. Preheat the oven to 350°F. Use the butter to grease an 8-inch square baking dish, then dust it evenly with the bread crumbs, knocking out the excess crumbs. Place a roasting pan with enough hot water to come halfway up the sides of the baking dish on the center oven rack.

2. In a large mixing bowl, combine the rice, milk, cream, salt, sugar, vanilla, eggs, and raisins, if using, and mix well. Pour into the prepared dish and place in the water bath. Bake until the custard is set and doesn't feel loose in the center, 30 to 40 minutes.

3. Let cool slightly, but serve warm.

ELLEN'S TIPS

★ You can use a mold for this dish, then unmold it when it is cool. If you do that, sprinkle the top with 1 tablespoon sugar mixed with a pinch of ground cinnamon, or some freshly grated nutmeg.

Sliced Summer Peaches
and Cream

Makes 6 servings

How can you beat a perfect peach? In summer, peaches are pure and sweet. Slice one and enjoy it with heavy cream and lots of sugar. Yum!

★ Half and half, heavy cream, or even cold milk is fine to serve with these peaches.

★ Room temperature for ripe fruit enhances the taste.

4 large ripe peaches
1 tablespoon fresh lemon juice
1 tablespoon granulated sugar

½ cup firmly packed light or
   dark brown sugar, for serving
1 cup cream, for serving

1. Place one peach at a time in a pot of boiling water for a few seconds. Remove it using tongs and peel under cold running water.
2. Cut the peaches in half, remove the pits, and slice. Place in a medium-size bowl and sprinkle with the lemon juice to keep them from turning brown. Sprinkle with 1 tablespoon of granulated sugar. Cover and keep at room temperature.
3. To serve, dish out each portion, then pass the brown sugar in a small serving bowl and the cream in a pitcher for guests to help themselves.

Index